Yemeni Pottery

Sarah Posey

Yemeni Pottery
The Littlewood Collection

Published for the Trustees of the British Museum
by British Museum Press

© 1994 The Trustees of the British Museum

Published by British Museum Press
A division of British Museum Publications
46 Bloomsbury Street
London
WC1B 3QQ

British Library Cataloguing in Publication Data
A catalogue record of this book is available from
the British Library

ISBN 0 7141 2512 1

Designed by Andrew Shoolbred
Typeset by Create Publishing Services Ltd, Bath, Avon
Printed in Great Britain by The Bath Press Ltd, Bath, Avon

Front cover: Water vessel (*sharbat-al-'arus*) and incense burner (*majmarah*). From left: cats 35 and 12.

Back cover: A woman buying pots from a stall-holder, Sanaa. (Photo: Carl Phillips, 1991).

1. (HALF TITLE PAGE) Water storage jars by the road to Dhala for the benefit of thirsty travellers. The jars are covered with wooden lids to keep out dirt and flies. An aluminium cup rests on the furthest pot.
(Photo: Mark Littlewood, 1960s)

2. (TITLE PAGE) Cooking pot (*burmah*). Cat. 80

3. (ABOVE) Incense burners (*majmarah*).
From left: cats 4, 1 and 2

Contents

Acknowledgements

I would like to thank a number of people for their help on this cata-logue: Imogen Laing for her ever-willing assistance at Orsman Road and Mike Row of the British Museum Photographic Service for the studio photographs; Andrew Middleton from Scientific Research and Venetia Porter from the Department of Coins and Medals for their most helpful comments; Carolyn Jones from the British Museum Press for her patience; Susanna Friedman of the BMP Production Depart-ment; and various colleagues in the Department of Ethnography for their constructive comments on earlier drafts of the text. I am also indebted to Carl Phillips, Ianthe Maclagan, Omar Mahdawi, June Posey, Nigel Hepper, Omar Bamatraf, Bilqis Bamatraf, and Idrees Al-Shammam of the Embassy of the Republic of Yemen for their insights, and Nigel Worlidge for his support. My special thanks go to Mark Littlewood who has been a fount of knowledge and has so generously given up his time to help at each stage of this project.

Both Mark Littlewood and I would especially like to thank Shelagh Weir. Without her encouragement Dr Littlewood would never have expanded his collection in the way that he did and the catalogue would not have come to fruition without her kind support and active in-volvement.

Foreword   by Mark Littlewood

The urge to collect was implanted in me when I was very young by a grandfather who later bequeathed to me his 'museum'—a cupboard filled with neatly labelled objects of 'material culture'. Some of these he had acquired after the Boer War and during the Great War of 1914–18, others during military tours of duty in India, Afghanistan and southern Africa.

While at school in Dorset I was greatly influenced by Donald Potter, the master responsible for sculpture and pottery, and I spent much time following the firing of the school kiln. It was from him that I learned to respect everyday objects and utensils that had been well made from natural materials—'craft' as opposed to 'art'.

So, when I arrived in Aden in 1961 to work as a medical officer at the oil refinery which had been constructed and was still, at that time, run by the British Petroleum Company, I was excited to find a wide range of domestic pottery on sale in the markets of Aden and in the neighbouring town of Shaykh Othman. Soon I set about acquiring examples of as many types of vessel as were available in Aden. Later the shopkeepers told me that some of their ware was being made for them by potters working at Mimdarah on the outskirts of Shaykh Othman, and in the neighbouring state of Lahej where there was a family of potters from Hays in north Yemen. They had settled on the edge of the capital, Al-Hauta (now known as Lahej), near to suitable clay deposits and a ready supply of fuel. Soon I was visiting these potters on a regular basis to observe the full cycle of manufacture: the digging of clay from the walls of a nearby *wadi* (water course); the 'puddling' and maturing of the clay under wet sacks; and the throwing, drying, glazing and firing—the whole process taking between one and two weeks.

It soon became obvious that the pottery on sale in Aden was not only made locally, but also included ware that had been imported from north Yemen, particularly from the southern capital of Taizz and also from what I later discovered were historic pottery towns on the coastal plain (the Tihamah). There potters known in Aden as 'Zabidis' (because they lived near the town of Zabid), had been making pots since medieval times. This was mostly glazed ware—the glaze made in recent years from the lead salts obtained from the electrodes of old car batteries, and often decorated with a copper–based slip which gave an attractive green colour against the golden yellow of the more usual lead glaze. Gradually I came to recognise the differing styles from the various centres; for example the ware from Rahidah in the foothills of the Tihamah which was burnished rather than glazed. As Aden at that time was still the centre of coastal trading by means of dhows and other craft, I often came across pots that had been brought in by seamen from such places as Berbera in Somalia, Socotra, and from places further east round the Arabian Peninsula: Mukalla, Oman, Ra's al-Khaymah, and even from as far away as Basra in Iraq.

Although my original plan had been to collect only such pots as could be acquired in and around Aden, as my interest in the subject became known, Yemenis who had been on holiday would bring me examples of pots from their home towns further afield. Also expatri-

4. Mark Littlewood with potters and their families, Lahej. (Photo: Mark Littlewood, 1960s)

ates visiting other parts of Arabia, remembering my enthusiasm, would bring back small examples, such as incense burners, from places they had visited.

Although my time with the oil refinery at Little Aden spanned a twelve-year period both before and after Independence, I was able to travel fairly freely around the Western and Eastern Aden Protectorate (as they were then called), in an old Land Rover with sand tyres. Also, as a doctor, I usually received a warm welcome at the various little villages we visited. In this way I used to come across small families of potters often using quite primitive methods of open firing and making their living under extremely difficult conditions. As in the Tihamah, the potters in the Wadi Hadramaut have a long tradition going back to medieval times; I only regret that my one visit to Tarim was too short to do more than acquire a few examples of their ware and take some photographs of their kilns.

As the collection increased, the problem arose as to what to do with it. Moving from house to house as the children increased in number, I was encouraged by my long-suffering wife to donate the collection to a museum. With some trepidation I therefore offered the first batch of pots to the Department of Ethnography of the British Museum where it was first received by Elizabeth Carmichael. She passed it on to her new colleague, Shelagh Weir, who expressed interest in the objects and

5. Typical Sanaa houses with raised clay decorations painted with lime-wash (*nurah*).
(Photo: Shelagh Weir, 1973–4)

encouraged me to build up the collection over the ensuing decade. This was one of her first involvements with Middle Eastern material, and I would like to think that it influenced her decision to specialise in this area.

After leaving Aden in 1972, I was seconded to various oil companies in the Gulf and had the opportunity to collect more pots in Qatar, Abu Dhabi, Sharjah and some of the smaller Emirates. Sadly, the sudden influx of oil wealth has brought little to encourage the pottery of Arabia apart from providing oil-soaked cardboard cartons which can be used as a cheap form of fuel for kilns.

I remain very grateful to my employers, the British Petroleum Company, who granted my family unlimited sea freight allowance. This generosity made the problem of shipping the pots to the UK merely a matter of careful packing.

I would also like to thank my friends and colleagues in Yemen, especially Mr Omar A. Bamatraf and Mr Mohammed Ahmed Dean, without whose help this collection would have been much less comprehensive.

6. Water vessels (*jarrah* or *kuz*). From left: cats 49, 54 and 53

Preface

The Littlewood collection of 181 pieces was made just prior to the period of rapid social and economic change in Yemen in the 1970s. It encompasses most types of domestic pottery still being made at that time, and illustrates the full range of techniques used to make and decorate the pots. Most of the pots were collected in and around Aden. Although the Aden area was more economically developed than the rest of the country in the 1960s and many of the changes which were to occur elsewhere in Yemen in the following two decades had already taken place, pots were still being made and traded there. Littlewood acquired examples in Aden itself, at Crater Market or from sailors at Ma'alla Harbour; in the town of Shaykh Othman, whose market primarily stocked the wares of potters based in the nearby pottery-making village of Mimdarah; and in the town of Lahej, which traded pots made both by potters based in the town itself and in local villages like Hamra to the east.

However, through a few expeditions further afield, and via friends travelling in north Yemen, Littlewood was also able to acquire examples of pottery from most of the main pottery-making centres along the Gulf of Aden coast, from the Wadi Hadramaut, and from the Tihamah which produces some of the finest contemporary ware. In the markets of Aden and Shaykh Othman, Littlewood also collected hand-made pottery items which had found their way from elsewhere in South Arabia, from the Middle East and from East Africa.

I took on the project of cataloguing the Littlewood collection with neither a specialist background in ceramics nor an in-depth knowledge of Yemen. However, I was immediately struck by the pots; by their distinctive and appealing shape and decoration and by the questions they raised about the culture which produced, traded and used them. I soon became intrigued also by two broader issues which emerged in the course of my research—the paucity of written material available on contemporary Yemeni pottery (and contemporary Yemeni crafts in general) and the Littlewood collection in the context of museum collecting.

Little has been written on contemporary Yemeni pottery, a curious omission for two reasons: first, because the pots are the product of a major South Arabian craft industry with a long history. Archaeologists have worked on sites in Yemen for several decades and research has been carried out on pottery material dating back to the fourth–fifth centuries BC. Since contemporary wares relate closely in manufacture, form and function to those in use in Yemen and further afield on the Syro-Palestinian coast during and since the last centuries of the first millennium BC, they provide valuable suggestions as to how the earlier examples may have been made and used. Olga Tufnell, an archaeologist and academic, was particularly interested in this area (Tufnell 1960 and 1961). She collected examples of both archaeological and contemporary pottery from south Yemen and organised an exhibition of the material at the Institute of Archaeology in London in 1960. However, sadly, her activities did not lead to much further research on contemporary Yemeni pottery, despite the amount of work carried out on the archaeological record since the time of her writings.

Secondly, items made of pottery play a central role in many important areas of contemporary Yemeni domestic and social life. Looking at water vessels, incense burners, coffee roasters, jugs and cups, smoking apparatus, cooking pots, braziers and toys can, therefore, teach us much about Yemeni culture and history.

The process of cataloguing the Littlewood collection of Yemeni pottery has provided a basis from which to explore these issues—to describe the craft of the potter and to examine the social context in which

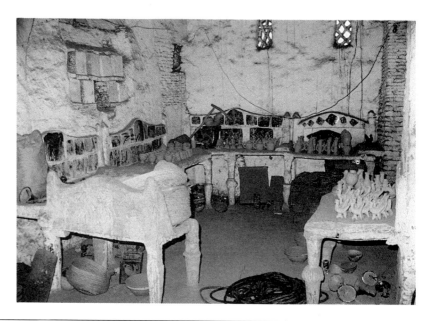

7. Interior of a potter's workshop in Hays with clay toys and pots laid out to dry. (Photo: Shelagh Weir, 1973–4)

the pots are made, traded and used. More generally it also highlights the way in which museums acquire their collections. The British Museum's Department of Ethnography is able to carry out its own fieldwork projects and acquire pieces for the collections as part of the process of long–term research in one area. However, to a great extent its collections are expanded through purchase and donation in Britain. In these cases, although the objects are valued additions to the Museum's holdings, they often come with little or no accompanying documentation other than their immediate history since acquisition abroad.

The Department was therefore fortunate to be offered the Littlewood pots since the collection is exceptional not only for the range of pots it contains, but also for the documentation which comes with them. Littlewood was particularly interested in how the pots were made. He became close friends with one potter in particular, Fitini Hazam, a young craftsman based just outside Lahej, and visited him regularly, documenting the various stages of manufacture and buying samples of his wares (see fig. 8). It is the detailed notes which Littlewood took in the 1960s and early 1970s when the collection was made, along with the small number of reports made around the same period (Tufnell 1960

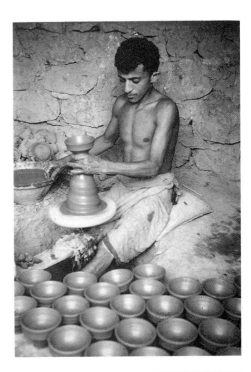

8. Fitini Hazam throwing small bowls from a larger lump of clay on a foot-operated fly-wheel set into a pit in the workshop floor, Lahej. (Photo: Mark Littlewood, 1960s)

and 1961, Champault 1974 and Weir 1975), which form the basis of this catalogue.

In collating this information many questions have emerged which remain to be answered, particularly relating to the social aspect of pot manufacture and use in Yemen in the 1960s and 1970s. For example, it would be interesting to learn more about women's involvement (or non-involvement) in pot-making, the use of certain designs and motifs to decorate the pots and their meaning (if any), and what Yemenis think about ceramic wares. With this in mind I hope that this catalogue will be useful as an introduction to Yemeni pottery and as a starting point for further research.

Both the technical section and the discussion of the use of the various types of pots relate to the period Littlewood spent in Yemen (1961–72). Although some of this data still applies to rural Yemen, there have been many changes in traditional practices since the pots were collected. The 'ethnographic present' used throughout this catalogue refers to the 1960s and 1970s.

Note on Transliteration, Terminology and Place Names

In the main text, the local Arabic terms for pottery have been transcribed as they are written rather than as they are pronounced. The Arabic *jim* has therefore been transcribed as 'j' although it is pronounced as a hard 'g' in much of southern Yemen including the Aden area. Diacritical signs have been used only in the Glossary.

The terms provided in this catalogue are mainly for pots made or used in the Aden area and the southern region of Yemen. However, it should be noted that different terms are sometimes used for pots of similar form and/or function in other parts of Yemen.

Diacritical signs have been omitted from place names, but the latter have been transcribed as accurately as possible. However, I have been unable to verify the correct transcription in every case.

Yemeni Pottery: Manufacture & Trade

Yemen

The Republic of Yemen lies in the south of the Arabian peninsula, bounded by Saudi Arabia and Oman to the north and east, the Red Sea to the west, and the Gulf of Aden to the south. The island of Perim in the Bab Al Mandab (the narrow strip of water between Yemen and the African mainland) and the island of Socotra in the Gulf of Aden are also part of Yemen (see map on p. 16).

Following the Civil War of the 1960s, the Yemen Arab Republic (YAR) was established in 1970 in north Yemen, replacing the centuries-old rule of the Imamate. The British had colonised Aden in 1839 and progressively expanded their control over the hinterland and what became the British Aden Protectorate. The People's Democratic Republic of Yemen (PDRY) was established in what had been the British-controlled territory in the south in 1967. The Republic of Yemen was formed in May 1990 with the unification of the former Yemen Arab Republic and the People's Democratic Republic of Yemen after a period of political unrest within and between the two countries in the 1970s and 1980s. As this catalogue goes to press the new Republic of Yemen has successfully held its first democratic general election.

Yemen has three main geographic and climatic zones: hot, arid coastal plains in the west and south; a mountainous interior with a sub-tropical or temperate climate and relatively high rainfall, especially in the western and southern parts; and desert regions in the east. There are no large, permanently flowing rivers, but there are many springs and wells, and narrow water courses and riverbeds (*wadis*) which run with water during the spring and summer rainy seasons. The most famous of these riverbeds is the fertile Wadi Hadramaut in eastern Yemen.

The population of the YAR was 9.3 million in 1986, and that of the PDRY 2.3 million in 1988. The total resident population of the united Republic of Yemen was estimated at around 11 million in 1990 (Central Statistical Organisation, 1991). Most of the population are settled agriculturalists, traders and artisans living in small villages and towns scattered throughout the highlands and coastal regions. Until the

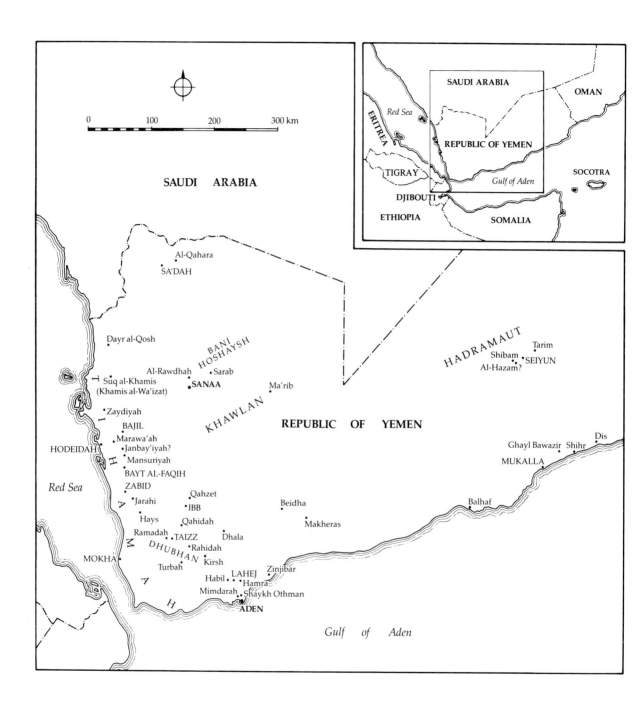

1970s rural communities were largely self-sufficient, living near sub-sistence level and relying mainly on locally-produced food and com-modities. Household utensils and personal possessions were few in number and simply made, largely by local craftsmen following cen-turies-old traditions. In many parts of the country there were no sur-faced or dirt-track roads, and the small number of items unavailable locally were traded from elsewhere in Yemen or imported from abroad and transported by donkey or camel.

The Yemeni economy was transformed in the 1970s mainly through the large-scale migration of Yemeni men, particularly from the north, to work in Saudi Arabia, and by the construction of roads and motor tracks. Wealth flowed back into Yemen in the form of remittances, and Yemenis began to acquire modern amenities. The great increase in cash incomes brought a leap in material aspirations and the develop-ment of a consumer society, sustained by a flood of imported com-modities. However, the oil-fed boom of the mid 70s–mid 80s is now over and the economic situation has worsened, particularly since the Gulf War in 1991 after which the majority of Yemeni migrant workers had to leave Saudi Arabia and return home.

The potters

Traditional Yemeni society is structured by a system of ranked social and occupational categories based on birth. At the bottom of this hier-archy is a minority of people considered to be of low status on account of their 'base' or unknown origins, or because they engage in occupa-tions considered demeaning or defiling by those above them in the social hierarchy. These occupations include petty market trading, the provision of certain services, especially those involving contact with polluting substances, and certain craft industries including pottery. Historically, the farmers, merchants and educated élite, who together formed the majority of the Yemeni population, would not intermarry with members of these low-status groups, reinforcing the latter's monopoly on their family-based professions. In at least one case, in the town of Tarim in the Wadi Hadramaut, this led to the development of a locally renowned 'guild' of hereditary potters. Despite the low social position of craftspeople such as potters in the Yemeni social hierarchy, they were given special protection under tribal customary law, and anyone who harmed them was obliged to pay especially high penal-ties. During the last twenty years there has been some erosion of these rigid hierarchies and their associated values as a consequence of the

9. Map of the Republic of Yemen, showing towns and villages mentioned in the text. (The position of smaller villages is only approximate, due to the lack of accurate maps of the country.) (Map: Graham Reed)

profound social and economic changes which have taken place throughout Yemen.

Potters can be found working in all regions of Yemen. Although there are some villages where several families earn their living from making and selling pots, most pottery is produced by a single potter or pottery-making family in any one village. Usually their production supplies a local demand only. Most potters are men, but in a few rural areas women potters work alongside them (as at Qahzet near Ibb and Sarab near Bani Hoshaysh). Children join in production at a young age; traditionally, the craft passes from generation to generation, a son learning from his father, or a nephew from an uncle. Workshops are always close to the potters' homes (or even inside the house), with kilns nearby. Within a village or local area a potter may become known for being particularly skilled at making one sort of pot, or in larger workshops an informal division of labour might develop as in Qahzet where the men and women carry out different aspects of the potting process. But, on the whole, any potter can turn his hand to whatever is demanded. It is interesting that Yemeni pottery production has not become more specialised and localised, with a greater division of labour and pots traded in quantity to the market. One clear barrier to such a development is the dispersal of the population over a large area and the difficult and diverse terrain that typifies Yemen.

10. Mohammed Qahtan (left) and a fellow Zabidi potter outside their workshop near Shaykh Othman. Before them are a range of water vessels drying in the sun. (Photo: Mark Littlewood, 1960s)

Potting is largely a full-time profession and is practised all the year round, although a potter may also grow vegetables and fruit for domestic consumption. However, Champault (1974) notes that, in some places in north Yemen, the large clay bread ovens are not made by professional potters but by certain village neighbours who have become known as talented oven-makers and are happy to provide this household item free of charge.

Workshops are usually set up close to suitable clay deposits and where there is a demand for pots from a reasonably-sized local population. There are few areas in Yemen without fairly easy access to deposits of clay. Potters may sometimes move away from their home village or town for a season or temporary period in response to market forces. The potters from Zabid are well known in Yemen as skilled craftsmen and some have settled far from their home in the Tihamah; for example, the Littlewood collection contains a number of 'Zabidi' pots made in Lahej. Historically Zabid was one of Yemen's major centres for pottery production (Mason and Keall 1988) although there are no potters based in the town today.

None of the pots in the Littlewood collection carry a potter's mark, as is the case with other craft products in Yemen which are not 'authored' in any way. However, Yemeni potters within the same locality easily recognise each other's work.

Making pots

The clay

Clay is obtained direct from the source, in some cases a cave, the *wadi* or riverbed in others, by the potter himself. Clay itself is not traded or transported over long distances; for the short journeys from the source to the pottery, the clay is either carried by the potters themselves, or heaped into baskets and (before motor transport) carried by donkey. It is covered by damp sacks to keep it workable, and stored in a hole in the ground or in the corner of the workshop.

The type of clay differs in quality and composition from region to region. The clay from Mimdarah near Shaykh Othman in Aden, for example, has a high salt content which makes it impossible to glaze, whereas that from Lahej is 'sweet' and salt-free. The pots from the Tihamah have a natural reddish tinge, as do those from the Hadramaut where the clay is also salty, unlike pots from Mimdarah where the clay is pale. And, while the clay from Dis and Shihr in the Hadramaut is very fine and smooth, the earth from Kabbat al-Shawush in the

11. Fitini Hazam kneading clay in preparation for use, Lahej. (Photo: Mark Littlewood, 1960s)

Tihamah is sandy. Mica deposits are evident in the clay from a number of different regions, and pieces of shell can be seen in some of Littlewood's examples from Rahidah (see cat. 65).

The clay is prepared in a number of ways before use. Tufnell (1961) records that in Tarim the pile of dry clay was first broken up with a mattock, then carefully washed in a trough. In other areas the new clay is soaked before being worked. In all cases a large mound of the freshly-prepared clay is laid on the floor, kneaded with the feet and foreign objects removed. Smaller pieces are then worked separately by hand (see fig. 11). In some areas it is sieved to make a fine, smooth paste appropriate for making smaller, more finely-wrought items. Alternatively, dung or straw can be worked into the clay, as in Tarim (see cat. 66). Sometimes dried or sifted dung is added to the clay in the process of making the pot (e.g. when beating). The addition of such 'non-plastics' gives the clay more 'body' and is appropriate for the making of larger pots. It also increases the clay's porosity, making the pot less liable to shrink while drying or to crack during firing. In one example in the Littlewood collection, hair (goat?) has been added to the clay to hold the pot together in its unfired state (see fig. 22, cat. 10).

Methods of manufacture

The five methods used by potters elsewhere in the world are all found in Yemen, often in combination with each other: modelling, coiling, moulding, beating and throwing.

Modelling is the simplest method: working the clay by hand from a solid lump. The toy animals in the Littlewood collection are examples of such work.

Coiled pots are formed out of a series of rolled lengths or 'sausages' of clay (see plate 2). Usually a flat base for the pot is first modelled or beaten into shape. The end of the first length of clay is attached around the edges of the base, the potter sealing the edges of the coil and base together with his fingers. He keeps coiling the length of clay around the rim of the pot, sealing the newest coil into that below, modelling the shape outwards or inwards as required, and either leaving the wall of the pot the same thickness as the coil or thinning it by extending the pot upwards. On some pots the ripple effect of the circling coils can be seen on the inside surface. On the outside the walls are smoothed by the potter's fingers or with a simple tool.

Yemeni potters will often use the base of a gourd or a completed vessel to mould the bottom of a pot. A lump of clay is shaped into a flat 'pancake' and pressed and beaten over or into the mould (see fig. 12). A length of sacking is often laid between the mould and the clay to prevent sticking and facilitate removal. The resulting bowl shape is smoothed with water and left to dry partially, to strengthen it before it is built up into the completed pot by coiling or beating. The necks of pots are often made with a cylindrical mould tapering slightly towards the top (see fig. 13). Again, flattened clay is worked around the mould before both neck and mould are inserted (tapered end first) into the small hole left in the top of the pot's body. The edge of the neck is joined at the edge of the hole and the mould removed.

Large vessels are made by beating a pot into the required shape. This method is also called 'paddle and anvil'. The pot is placed on a stand. The potter holds a stone (often with a convex surface) or just his fist inside the vessel against the inner wall, as he works his way around the pot beating the outer surface quickly and evenly with a wooden paddle (often with a concave surface) held in his other hand (see plate 1). Rolls of clay are worked into the walls of the pot as it is built up. The potter usually has a selection of different bats, from thick and heavy to thin and light, with which to work the clay at the various stages in the pot's manufacture. The paddle is usually corrugated and the resulting 'combed' effect which is transferred to the surface of the pot is often left unsmoothed as decoration (see fig. 14). Some large water jars or cooking vessels with rounded bases are worked upside down. The pot is rested on its neck and its belly is rounded and worked inwards until the hole fits the potter's wrist and finally his finger. The tiny opening is then closed with a piece of clay and the lightest paddle. Water jars sometimes have a 'ring' base added so that they can stand. Bread ovens are beaten into shape from a lump of clay modelled into a basic hollow cylinder. When using the paddle and anvil method the potter may simply sit with the vessel in his lap, turning it as he works. Larger pots are mounted on a support, such as a square piece of wood on a basket full of earth or an upturned pot, and the potter walks around the vessel as he works.

Some pots are made by being thrown on a rudimentary potter's wheel revolved by a foot-operated flywheel (see fig. 8). The wheel is used to throw smaller items such as cups and bowls. Items are often formed one after the other from the top of a large solid cylinder of clay on the wheel and each cut off with a wire as it is completed. One man can make up to 400 small bowls in a day's work by this technique. The potters of Zabid are said to be especially skilled at this method, and the town was noted for its wares as early as the fourteenth century (Tufnell 1960). In the Aden potteries, the wheel is set into a pit in the hut floor, whereas in Mukalla it is mounted in the open on a stand and in Hays on

12 and 13. A female potter in Rawdha, near Sanaa.
Left: shaping a flat 'pancake' of clay over a convex mould to form the base of a pot.
Right: forming the neck of a pot using a cylindrical mould. The neck will be attached to the base of the water jar resting at her feet. (Photos: Shelagh Weir, 1973–4).

a stand in the workshop. In all cases a central column of stone or wood turns in a bearing which is set into the ground. The column passes through a hole in the centre of the stone kick-wheel which the potter rotates with his foot, while working the clay on a smaller stone or circular stone and mud turntable set on the rotating spindle. The potter sits on the ground in those cases where the wheel is set into a pit, or on a crude seat mounted on a wooden column, one of two upright pillars set into a wooden plank which supports the wheel, where it is free-standing.

In some potteries, such as those in Shibam and Tarim in the Hadramaut, this kind of wheel is not used but, as in Al-Qahara north of Sa'dah, a more basic turn-table can be made by placing the clay on a flat stone balanced on a domed stone. The flat stone is revolved slowly by hand while the pot is worked into shape.

The process of making a pot can take several days and involve several stages. In Sharj near Mukalla, Tufnell (1961) reports that it took two days to make a large water jar where the vessel is built up by coiling, section by section. The 15 cm diameter base was set on the ground, and each section was added 10 cm at a time then left to dry for about two hours. The coiling and drying process was repeated until the jars were built up to their full height of 70 cm.

14. Water vessel (*jahlah*). Cat. 62

Decoration

Yemeni pots are decorated in various ways and at different stages in their manufacture. Large water jars are seldom painted or heavily decorated but may simply be incised with simple flecks or lines around the neck and rim when the clay has partially dried. Smaller water vessels are more frequently incised and may have patterns covering much of the surface area (see fig. 16). The designs are broadly similar to the painted decorations described below, featuring linear designs, striped and cross-hatched areas, and also wavy bands. Alternatively some small items such as incense burners have a stamped design applied to the surface (see fig. 17). These feature 'flower', 'leaf' and circular designs. There are only a few examples in the Littlewood collection of pieces that are both incised or stamped, and washed with a slip or glaze.

Some smaller vessels for water and coffee are burnished with a quartz pebble or shell before the pot is completely dry (see fig. 15). The burnishing increases the pot's capacity to hold liquid, by contrast with the untreated surface of the large water storage jars, the porosity of which helps keep their contents cool.

Once dry, the pot may be covered with a slip, a homogeneous mixture of sieved clay and water, varying in tone from an off-white or buff to a rust-red. A slip of the same type of clay used to make the pot provides an even surface to the piece, or an alternative clay slip can be used to create a different surface tone, contrasting with the base clay if

15. A female potter in Mansuriyah, near Hodeidah, burnishing vessels before they are completely dry.
(Photo: Shelagh Weir, 1973–4)

applied partially (see fig. 38). Designs may also be painted on with a slip, or slips of contrasting tone, either directly onto the dried pot or over a previously applied slip (eg. figs 27 and 41). These designs consist largely of linear patterns, although some 'flower' and 'leaf' motifs are also used. Triangular and oblong areas of cross-hatched colour feature on many of the pots, alternating with areas of plain colour. Once fired, the slip washes and decoration hold fast to the surface of the pot. (However, in some of the under-fired examples, the slip has not been properly fixed and rubs off when touched.)

Pots can also be decorated in a number of ways after firing. Many of the pots in the Littlewood collection are washed with *nurah*, a solution made of lime ground from lumps of limestone which the potters buy and mix with water. (The same mixture is used for house-painting, see fig. 5.) It is applied to pieces not previously washed or decorated with slip. Once dried, it provides a bright white base for further decoration. (Almost none of the pots are left unadorned once lime-washed.) Designs are painted on using either different shades of slip or the bright chemical colours of imported Quink pen ink in yellow, purple, blue, green, red and black (see fig. 3). These inks, and the availability of purple, blue and green colours, are relatively recent innovations for

16. Water vessels (*sharbat al-'arus*). From left: cats. 37, 136 (miniature version) and 32

the Yemeni potter. Traditionally, the few colours used were made from natural pigments; black from a mixture of soot and oil, and shades of red and yellow from earth ochres.

The brides' water jars (*sharbat al-'arus*) (see figs 16 and 32) and incense burners, are examples of these more highly decorated pots. Although the Quink ink is indelible and dries hard, neither the lime-wash nor unfired slip designs 'fix' to the surface of the pot, so rub off when touched. Incense burners are not handled to the same extent as, for example, cooking pots, and the *sharbat al-'arus* is purely decorative and non-functional. This may explain why it is these pots rather than other types which are decorated in this way. The lower part of some of the larger, plainer water storage jars is also coated with lime-wash. Tufnell (1961) claims that this is to reduce porosity.

A further pigment worth noting, used to decorate pots on Socotra Island, is 'dragon's blood', a red-coloured resin obtained from *Dracaena cinnibari*. The ripe fruit of the tree is coated with a resinous exudation, giving, when dried and ground, a fine red powder which dissolves in alcohol and other organic solvents. It is used in many parts of the world as a colouring varnish and lacquer, principally on metals, and has a distinctive sheen when painted onto the pots (see plate 6). It has been used in South Arabia since ancient times as a pigment and medicinal commodity. *Kohl* or antimony is also used, though infrequently, to colour the surface of pots, giving a metallic lustred effect. In an example from the Littlewood collection, the powder has been rubbed over an incised and lime-washed piece (see fig. 39).

The incised and painted designs are largely linear, made up of areas of cross-hatched lines, and triangles and squares of colour. It has been suggested that much pottery, from all over the world, draws on basketry for its form and decoration (Cooper 1981), and it is possible that the cross-hatching, contrasting areas of diagonal lines and decorative ridges on Yemeni pots hark back to the weave on baskets. Some pots also carry designs of wavy lines, dots, circles and flowers, although almost all the images are non-representational. The exceptions in the Littlewood collection are the fine birds surmounting four of the incense burners from Shaykh Othman and Lahej (see fig. 17).

A small number of pots are decorated with pieces of clay applied to the surface of the pot (see fig. 28). The Littlewood collection has no examples of pots with decorative pieces of clay, sometimes in the shape of birds, hanging on wire from the handles of water pots (which exist in other collections), although one unfired incense burner has droplets of clay hanging from its sides on cotton thread (see fig. 3).

Only a small number of pots, mainly those from Hays in the Tihamah, are glazed. Indeed potters in Hays have been producing glazed ware for at least four centuries (Keall 1983) and some of the finest pieces of the medieval period came from this major centre. Today most of these are mixing bowls, coffee pots and cups, which have been partially covered with a lime-wash and lead-based glaze. The lead for the 'flux' of the glaze is today obtained from car batteries, ground to a powder on a stone rotary quern, sieved through a woman's muslin veil and mixed to a paste with water before being added to the slip. The glaze varies in colour from a pale yellow through a greeny-mustard to dark green and brown, depending on the amount of iron (yellow/red when oxidised) or copper (green when oxidised), taken from car battery plates, in the slip. One of the drinking cups illustrated (see plate 5) shows how different lead glazes are used decoratively to create areas of contrasting colour. An unusual and elaborate incense burner has been glazed a fine shiny yellow (see fig. 18), and two other incense burners in the collection are also glazed (cats. 14 and 15).

The relationship between the method of manufacture of a pot and its decoration is interesting. It seems that few, if any, of the pots made on a wheel are decorated other than with a lead glaze; painted, incised and added decorations seem to be restricted to hand-built examples.

17. BELOW LEFT Incense burners (*majmarah*). Left, cat. 24; right, cat. 18

18. BELOW RIGHT Incense burner (*majmarah*). Cat. 13

Only four pieces in the Littlewood collection are non-wheel made but glazed—the incense burners referred to above and a small bust of a man (see fig. 29). Littlewood comments that they are untypical.

Firing

Before firing, the pots are left to dry, either slowly in the shade of the workshop or more quickly in the sunshine (see fig. 10). The pot from Sharj described above was left to dry in the open for ten days before firing, whereas it only takes eight hours to dry small cups under similar conditions—the larger pots have to be dried more slowly to avoid cracking. The largest water jar from Mimdarah was left to dry for twenty days under cover.

The kilns are simply made. Those from Aden, Mukalla and the Hadramaut are updraft kilns consisting of a cylindrical structure built of mud and stone, some 1 to 1.5 m high. Fuel is fed into a lower compartment and the pots loaded into the upper section from the top. The hot gases are drawn upwards into the dome where they escape through a hole in the chimney. Tufnell (1961) describes an example in Sharj near Mukalla. It was filled with sixteen large jars, without dividers between them, with smaller pots filling the gaps, and piled directly on top of the fuel below. The mouth of the kiln was covered with broken shards and the lower compartment fuelled with camel dung. In Tarim, and also in Hays, it seems that the potters took greater

19. Potters preparing an updraft kiln in Zinjibar. The kiln, made of mud and stone, has been packed with pots from the top and sealed with old potsherds. Fuel is being fed through a side opening to the left.
(Photo: Mark Littlewood, 1960s)

care in firing their wares, loading the pots onto a grid supported on columns which raised the pots clear of the fire. A space was left between each item, the mouth of the kiln sealed with over a foot of clay and the stoke hole similarly sealed. In Tarim the firing took between four to five hours for each batch and was fuelled with brushwood or dung since wood is scarce and valuable for other purposes. In Shaykh Othman, Littlewood observed that the firings in similar updraft kilns took only two hours—the kilns were again fuelled with brushwood brought from the desert by camel. In Qahzet, near Ibb, kilns were large open-roofed rectangular structures sufficient to hold about ten ovens. At Marawa'ah near Hodeidah, and nearby Mansuriyah and Dayr al-Qosh, Weir (1975) describes the firing of pots in large pits dug in the ground and sometimes lined with mud. The pots were placed in the pit with the fuel, covered with potsherds and rubble and then fired. At Hamra, near Lahej, pots were also fired in pits, the pots piled on top of each other and the brushwood fire lighted over them. In some areas palm branches and the fuel-impregnated cardboard packing of oil cartons were also burned. It is unclear what effect these different firing methods have on the pots.

In many cases the firing of pots is a fairly 'hit-and-miss' affair; in badly-packed kilns many pots may break, and with the more crude kilns it is difficult to control the temperature of the firing. In the firings witnessed by Tufnell at Sharj, only half the pots survived, although some of the split and warped examples were 'made good' when cooled by a heavy coating of white lime plaster (a thicker version of the lime-wash described above). Another result of overpacking pots into a kiln is the appearance of 'fire-clouds' or 'flashing' on the surface of the clay where two pots have touched and the chemicals in the clay have not oxidised sufficiently (see fig. 37, cat. 74). The resulting dark markings can often have a decorative effect and are indeed a recognised and desired feature of certain types of pottery in other countries. The temperatures reached by the Yemeni kilns are probably relatively low, between 600°–1,000° C, evidenced by the softness of the clay even after firing. Temperatures vary greatly between kilns and within the kiln between one position and another and from one moment to the next. However, low-temperature firing favours resistance to 'thermal shock', making this method particularly useful for cooking pots, incense burners and pipe-bowls which experience direct heat in use. One of the defining factors of a successful firing would seem to be the ability to control the temperature of the kiln, both in terms of reaching a given temperature and sustaining the heat over a given time. The potters in Yemen are not in a position to predict the supply, source and quantity of their fuel, by far the most expensive element in the pot-making process. They must make do with whatever is available at the time and do not have the luxury of being able to experiment with their fuel so as to be sure of the result of any given firing. The lack of fuel may also explain the tendency to overpack the kilns. With fuel as a scarce and expensive commodity, it is more economic to overpack a kiln and take the risk of losing up to half the pots, than only to pack half the pots in the first place.

It is likely that one or two items in the Littlewood collection were fired in a domestic oven or simply sun-baked (see fig. 22, cat. 10). These would not hold water or sustain much use.

Trade

Aden is a major trading centre, not only for imported goods, but also for commodities brought from various parts of Yemen and traded for both domestic use and export.

Thus, at the period Littlewood made his collection (and still today), some pots from major pottery centres elsewhere in Yemen were traded to Aden, particularly the characteristic glazed wares from Hays. These were imported primarily for sale to Adenis, although some Haysi wares, often made by Haysi potters based in or around Lahej, were

20. Pots and bread ovens (*tannur*) (right) on sale in Shaykh Othman. The larger pieces are packed and carried in the reed baskets.
(Photo: Mark Littlewood, 1960s)

traded to Shaykh Othman and even on to Djibouti and Berbera across the Red Sea. Other key ports along the Gulf Coast and Red Sea were also busy trading centres for pots. Mukalla, 300 miles to the east of Aden, sold pots from the nearby village of Dis and from the open-air pottery at Shihr. Tarim, the ancient centre of learning in the Hadramaut, had a large community of potters whose wares were also sold at the market of Seiyun, a larger town close by. Tufnell (1961) reports that the needs of Shibam, slightly to the south in the Hadramaut, were met by the potters in Al-Hazam. In the Tihamah, Hays was, and remains, well known for its glazed wares which are traded throughout Yemen. Pots from some of the Tihamah pottery centres were often traded as far as the highland town of Taizz to the east, whose market also sold wares from Ramadah and Rahidah.

However, pottery manufacture usually served a local demand; since the items were fragile, widely available from the large number of local potters and cheap in price, they were not a practical commodity to transport over long distances and difficult terrain. In most cases the pots which travelled did so as gifts rather than as trade items, although this situation has changed somewhat with motor transport.

For transportation the pots were strung together on a wood frame (see fig. 21), packed in baskets or wrapped two or three together in matting bags and carried by donkey or camel. Unlike other craft items in Yemen which were traded by professional merchants, the potters themselves, or members of their family, sold their wares direct from the pottery or at the hundreds of weekly markets held in local villages

21. Seven jugs (*masabb*). Cat. 69

and towns all over the country (see fig. 20). In some cases professional traders took selected items on to more distant markets.

Also included in the Littlewood collection (but not catalogued here since they fall outside the strict definition of Yemeni pottery) are pottery items traded to Aden and Shaykh Othman from elsewhere in South Arabia, the Middle East and East Africa. Often these were not pieces traded in quantity but were offered to Adeni merchants by sailors who brought the pots to sell for extra cash. Some were transported from the Arab Gulf by dhow, including such pieces as the finely worked and decorated incense burners from Sallala in Oman which were popular gifts among Adenis and very similar to pieces made in Mukalla. Also from Oman came unadorned incense burners in a distinctive red clay. From further north are three incense burners, a water vessel, two cooking pots and an ornate serving dish from Dubai, simple cup-style incense burners from Bahrain, and white water jars from Basra in Iraq. Traded more widely in Yemen are the distinctive incense burners, braziers and pipe-bowls from Somalia, carved from soft, white stone, and from Ethiopia come finely-worked small jugs, burnished to a high sheen in black or orange clay with incised decoration. Particularly curious are the clay animals from Baluchistan which are similar to those made in Yemen, the latter in turn closely resembling in form and decoration those made in ancient times.

With the exception of the more decorative items described in the 'Making pots' section above, such as certain water pots and incense burners, Yemeni pots were cheap to buy and easily broken, providing a steady market but a low income for the Yemeni potter. Rather than being a deliberate 'built-in obsolescence', the fragility of the pots would seem to be a function of the resources the potter has to hand, particularly the scarcity and expense of fuel for the kilns which results in low-fired and vulnerable wares.

PLATE 1 A textile dyeing workshop in Zabid. The indigo vats are large, ceramic jars. (Photo: Shelagh Weir, 1973-4)

PLATE 3 *(Overleaf)* Water vessel *(sharbat al-'arus)*. Cat. 36

PLATE 2 Potters in Mansuriyah, near Hodeidah. The man is building up the coil pots from a series of rolled lengths of clay. The woman is decorating wares with black slip or ink. (Photo: Shelagh Weir, 1973-4)

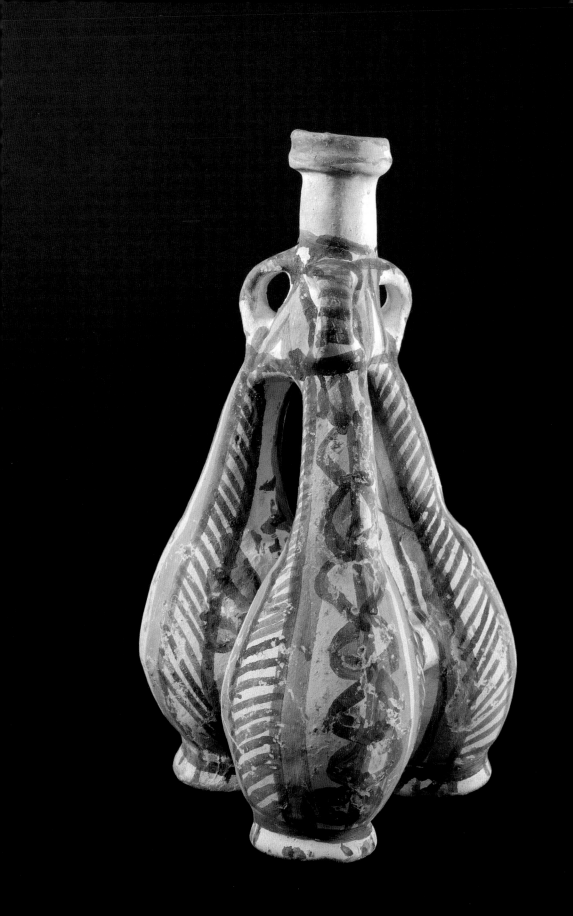

The Place of Pottery in Yemeni Culture

Incense burners

Incense has been traded and used in South Arabia for about 3000 years. The legend of the Queen of Sheba reflects the power and wealth of the kingdoms in northern Yemen which engaged in the long-distance trade in incense between South Arabia and Egypt, Mesopotamia, Greece, Rome, India and even China. However, the trade for which the region became famous ended in the fourth century AD, principally due to the spread of Christianity, to the economic decline of Rome and to warring between South Arabian states.

The term 'incense' covers a variety of gums, resins and spices which emit a fragrance when burned or evaporated. More specifically, the term refers to the particular gums and resins which form the principal ingredients: frankincense and myrrh. It is these two commodities which were once traded the 1700 km length of the Arabian peninsula in antiquity.

Frankincense and myrrh trees favour different environments from each other. The frankincense tree (*Boswellia sacra*) grew only in south Yemen where it can still be found in the coastal mountains of the Hadramaut. The myrrh tree (*Commiphora myrrha*) only ever flourished in north Yemen and favours lower level escarpments. It still grows on the road from Taizz to Zabid.

The sap is tapped, once or even twice a year, to obtain the oily liquid and is often mixed with a gum or resin to solidify the incense and prevent it from evaporating. Small pieces are then chipped off the block of incense and may be powdered or ground before being sprinkled on the charcoal embers in braziers (on which coffee and food are also kept warm), or in specially-made incense burners which contain embers from a brazier or the kitchen oven.

As in the past, incense is still a relatively expensive commodity, used in the home primarily during social gatherings and certain religious festivals, or presented as a gift. There are numerous kinds and blends of incense available for sale in Yemen today, each with its own term and use on particular occasions, and a number of varieties are imported from India, Singapore and Indonesia. At gatherings, the

22. Incense burners (*majmarah*). Left, cat. 10; right, cat. 12

incense burner is often passed from guest to guest, each person receiving it with their right hand, drawing it close to their face and waving the vapour to their nose with their left hand while praising the host. In some areas of Yemen, incense is wafted underneath a visitor's gown as in the Gulf, or clothes are scented by being draped across a special wicker frame over an incense burner before they are worn. It is also used to perfume certain water jars before use, as described in the 'Water' section. In some rural areas incense is burned, particularly in the early morning and at sunset, as protection against the 'evil eye'. In the ancient world incense was included in prescriptions for a variety of ailments and it also has a number of medicinal uses in present-day Yemen. Incense is also used domestically as a deodoriser.

Today some Yemenis use electric incense burners imported from Japan, although others claim that they spoil the odour of the incense and burn the chips too quickly, and some recent examples of the traditional pottery incense burners are decorated with chemical paints and varnished rather than burnished. To some extent cologne has taken the place of incense at the end of social gatherings in the home, when it is sprayed on guests after meals and as they depart.

Incense is only one element in a range of resins, oils, herbs and spices which are used as perfumes and deodorisers in Yemen; for example, locally-produced sandalwood and a variety of scented oils are also burned for similar purposes. In certain parts of Yemen herbs, particularly basil, are grown, and are worn by women in bunches in their scarves, exchanged as gifts or pounded, as in the case of turmeric, for use as a skin cream.

Incense burners (*majmarah*) are amongst the more brightly-decorated ceramic items in the Littlewood collection, probably because they are used for the conspicuous consumption of a precious commodity. They are mostly lime-washed and then painted, often using pen inks in red, yellow, black, blue, green and purple. There are also a number of glazed examples. There are two main forms, each with variations: the 'cup' style resembles a miniature brazier, on a stem, often with a handle; the 'covered' style usually has a main opening with a number of decorative ventilation holes and one or two handles. This latter kind is used when perfuming clothes, the 'cover' protecting the gowns from the hot coals on which the incense is burned.

Water vessels

Yemenis distinguish between different kinds of water, not only with regard to the way the water will be used (i.e. whether for drinking, washing, ritual ablutions and so on), but also according to the quality of drinking water. Good water is described as 'light' on the stomach, and sayings in north Yemen express the belief that good water affects not only one's health but also dialect and eloquence. As a result Yemenis will often travel far to fetch supplies of drinking water from a renowned spring or well. Good drinking water is considered particularly important during *qat* sessions when the chewing of the *qat* makes the mouth dry and creates a strong thirst. (*Qat* is the Arabic term for the mildly stimulant leaves of the shrub *Catha edulis* Forssk. which is

23. Girls filling water jars from a well on the road north of Zaydiyah. The jars will be transported home by donkey. (Photo: Shelagh Weir, 1973–4).

cultivated in the Yemeni highlands. Most *qat* is chewed by men at their afternoon social gatherings and also features at women's afternoon tea-parties (*tafritah*) in certain areas.)

Until relatively recently, all water for use in the home had to be fetched daily by the women of the household. In the strict sexual division of labour, fetching water from wells and springs was, and remains, an exclusively female task (although men now transport large quantities in trucks). Traditionally water was carried from its source in pottery jars or gourds, although now plastic buckets or metal jerry-cans are used. Water containers were either carried on the woman's head, sometimes supported by a head-ring, or strapped into net bags or baskets and transported by donkey (see fig. 23). In rural areas fetching water remains one of women's most time-consuming and arduous tasks, as sources of water are often far from settlements through mountainous terrain. Most of the larger towns now have piped water and villagers in many areas now store water for household use in sheet-metal water tanks. In the Aden area, these tanks were formerly filled from a water trailer pulled by a camel, but today they are serviced by special pick-up trucks carrying water tanks, as they are throughout Yemen. Everywhere domestic water is stored in metal tanks, while for convenience water for drinking and ablutions is often still stored in two or three large pottery jars.

In some areas of Yemen, the storage jars for drinking water are perfumed before use. The larger vessels are upturned over an incense burner until the scented smoke permeates the pot, while the incense burner itself is placed inside smaller vessels until the pot has filled with smoke. The large storage vessels stand in the kitchen, yard and bathroom, and all storage jars are kept permanently filled with water. Since they are unglazed and therefore porous, the water evaporates on the surface of the pot, keeping the water cool in all weathers. The smaller jars are used to fill the larger vessels, and jugs or cups are used as scoops.

In Aden, the smaller pots were scrubbed inside and out with a coconut fibre brush and the larger ones with sand and palm fibres. In some areas Yemenis keep the green mould which grows on the outside base of a water storage jar for the treatment of small wounds on the hands and legs of their children.

Nowadays drinking water is usually brought into the living room in thermos flasks and drunk from glasses, or bottled mineral water is bought. Sometimes a child is sent out to fetch canned soft drinks to impress guests during *qat* sessions.

The large number of water vessels in the Littlewood collection includes the large-, medium- and small-sized water storage jars and jugs used in Yemen. The largest storage jar (*zir*) holds up to 50 litres of water approximately, the medium-sized jar (*jahlah*) up to 20 litres, and the small-sized jars (*kuz* and *jarrah*) up to one litre each. The openings of the *zir* and *jahlah* are covered with a wooden lid or metal plate and the jars themselves are kept on a wooden stand, with a small bowl beneath to catch any leakage from the vessel. The *kuz* and *jarrah* sit on a metal dish and often stand in a specially-made window to benefit from the cooling breeze. They are covered with an upturned metal or ceramic cup. Some kinds of jug (*jamanah*), often the burnished examples, are used for coffee as well as water, the same form serving two functions (e.g. cat. 44). However, once used for water or coffee the pot always retains the same function. Particularly striking are the decorative water vessels (*sharbat al-'arus*) which would have formed part of the 'trousseau' that a bride takes to her new home. These are less commonly seen today and may have been commissioned pieces. Two further types of water vessel with special functions are the pots used to carry drinking water to the fields (the *jamanah* again), and the smallest pots (*ibriq*) containing water for ritual ablutions which have a spout to direct the water. A lidded storage vessel was inspired by fourteenth-century Chinese imports to Yemen, a popular style amongst Yemeni potters particularly during the thirteenth to fifteenth centuries when many such pots were traded to Yemen (Tufnell 1960). (See fig. 24.) There are a number of examples listed under the 'Water' section of the catalogue that may in fact have had more general uses for food and oil.

All the water vessels are unglazed but the smaller ones are often highly decorated, either with bright paints, as in the case of the *sharbat al-'arus*, or with intricate incised designs and cross-hatching.

Food preparation and consumption

The speed with which food is consumed and the unvarying character of most Yemenis' diet belies the importance of food preparation and consumption in Yemeni society.

Women take considerable time and care over the preparation of meals and snacks. The main meal is served at midday. Although the menu of any meal is fairly predictable, the ingredients and the kinds and amounts of spices used and the way in which a dish is put together and cooked all conform to detailed recipes. Yemenis know the dishes well, and have developed a critical taste which expects the highest

24. Vessel, possibly for water storage, although it may have been intended for purely decorative use. Cat. 73

standards for traditional meals. Meals are carefully balanced, and are seen in particular as counteracting the effects of *qat*; *qat* is seen as 'cooling' and 'drying', so meals must be 'hot' and 'moistening' (Weir 1985). Food is central to hospitality, and it is an indicator of a man's status if his household can provide food for guests or make gifts of food to friends, neighbours or the needy. However meals are not lingered over; instead, the afternoon *qat* parties for men, and women's tea parties (*tafritah*) (and also *qat* parties in some areas), are the forums for socialising. Generally, in Yemen there is not a culture of eating out at restaurants as a way of socialising; restaurants and cafés mainly provide for men working away from home.

Food is prepared exclusively by women, either in a kitchen located in a corner of a household's compound in coastal villages, or on an upper floor of a multi-storeyed house in the highlands. Traditionally the kitchen is a hot, dark, smoky and spartan place, inadequately ventilated through a hole in the ceiling above the stove, and through one or two small windows. In most areas kitchens have at least one bread oven (*tannur*)-*cum*-stove, consisting of a large pottery cylinder set into a bench made of clay. The ovens are fuelled with small pieces of kindling wood inserted into an opening near the base. One or two metal crossbars are laid across the top to support cooking pots or the large flat clay plate (*malahhah*) for the preparation of sorghum-flour pancakes. Bread is baked by slapping flat rounds of dough onto the sides of the oven. More recently, many people have installed butane gas ovens and separate burners to supplement or replace the traditional wood-fuelled bread oven.

Food is usually eaten in one of the main living rooms—by the men first if guests are present, *en famille* if not. The dishes are laid out on a cloth or plastic mat on the floor with people squatting round.

The staple food in Yemen is bread. Bread made from a variety, or often a combination, of grains, including wheat, barley, sorghum, lentils and other legumes, is baked at least once a day. The basis of any meal in Yemen is bread and relish, which varies from a vegetable stew or broth to milk or ghee, although rice is increasingly served as part of the main midday meal throughout Yemen. Meat is the principal prestige food item, formerly only presented on special occasions or when entertaining, but now eaten more frequently. The midday meal usually includes the national dish of *hilbah*, a broth made from fenugreek flour, leeks, chillies and garlic into which bread is dipped. Meat and other dishes accompany it or follow it. There are regional variations in diet, but Yemeni cuisine generally employs a wide variety of spices and herbs: garlic, chillies, thyme, coriander, cardamom, cinnamon, cloves, cumin, ginger, mint and parsley. In most areas sweet food, such as cakes or bread soaked in butter and honey, is served only on special occasions, and usually at the start of the meal. Apart from mutton broth, nothing is drunk with a meal, and only in certain regions is tea or coffee served afterwards.

In many areas of Yemen food is often served in the vessel it was cooked in. Traditional cooking pots are either of grey steatite stone (these are more prevalent in the north), or round-bottomed pots (*burmah*) of clay. Stone vessels retain heat more effectively and are less likely to break. For these reasons, and because they are much more difficult and time-consuming to make, they are far more expensive, cherished and carefully mended than those made of clay, which are easily and cheaply replaced when broken. Dishes are brought to the eating area where individuals scoop up mouthfuls from the communal pot with their right hands, also using pieces of bread or pancake to hold the food and soak up the broth. In Aden, Indian-made metal cooking utensils and containers have been in use for the last fifty years or so, and aluminium pots and pans have been in common use throughout the country since the 1970s. However, in rural areas, they have supplemented rather than replaced those of pottery and stone.

In addition to the stoves and ovens, mixing bowls and cooking pots, every kitchen has a range of wooden and metal spoons, skewers, scoops and a rolling-pin or mortar and pestle for crushing herbs and spices. At one time, every kitchen had a quern for grinding grain, but since the introduction of motorised flour mills in the past few decades, almost all flour is now mechanically ground.

25. Bowls (*maqla*).
From left: cats 97, 98 and 96

The Littlewood collection features both partially glazed and unglazed mixing bowls (*harad* and *sayniyyah* are partially glazed examples), a cup, cooking pots (*burmah*), a pancake platter (*malahhah*), plates (*sahn*) and dishes (*maqla*), jugs, and a number of braziers (*marbakh*) for keeping prepared dishes or pots of coffee warm. The *sayniyyah* is used for soup and sour milk. The *burmah* and *malahhah* are treated with oil over the stove before they are first used, to seal their porous, unglazed surface. A pierced, conical tin lid covers the *malahhah* while the sorghum pancake cooks. The *sahn* is for eating from and is most commonly used for finger millet flour (*dukhn*). The pots and braziers are either unadorned, decorated with a few incised lines or partially glazed.

Smoking

Adults of both sexes smoke the water-pipe, mainly in segregated social gatherings. As in many Middle Eastern countries, sharing the water-pipe is an important social activity and plays a central role during afternoon gatherings. The activity binds the group as the hose of the pipe is passed from guest to guest.

Yemen's main tobacco-growing areas are Ghayl Bawazir, between Mukalla and Shihr on the Hadramaut coast, and the Tihamah. Tobacco

26. A *qat* party in Sanaa. Note the two water-pipes (*mada'ah Muneibari*) with clay pipe-bowls, and the several thermos flasks. The latter have increasingly replaced pottery jars for the serving of water on such occasions. (Photo: Shelagh Weir, 1973–4)

from these regions is exported to the Arab World and provides an important source of foreign currency. Tobacco leaves are also imported from India and often mixed with date syrup (though not for *qat* parties). Cigarette smoking is also popular among men.

A water-pipe is made up of a number of elements. With the *mada'ah Muneibari* the water container is made from a coconut imported from India encased in decorative metalwork, which has lent its name to whatever kind of vessel (pottery or metal) now performs this function, as well as to the entire smoking apparatus. Those made of pottery are particularly effective since they keep the water at a low temperature and cool the smoke more efficiently as it is drawn through. The decorated coconut (*habba*) is often mounted on an ornate brass tripod stand. Attached to the top opening is a long stem (*qutb*) of brass or turned wood (usually oak) inlaid with white metal, with a fitted decorative brass support for the hose. (The length of tube which fits inside the *habba* and sits in water is named *bulbula* after the *bulbul* nightingale, since the gurgling of the water when the pipe is being smoked is said to resemble the bird's song.) The top end of the stem is made completely of metal and is surmounted by a pottery pipe-bowl (*buri*). Lighted coals from a brazier are placed in the pipe-bowl and the tobacco leaves are laid on top. A wire mesh is sometimes placed around the *buri* in case the pottery should crack with the heat, and just below it the metal stem flares out into a small dish to catch any falling coals. The *buri* can also be covered with a conical pierced tin lid for the same purpose. A length of decorated wooden pipe (*mashab*) is attached to the side opening of the *habba*, from which coils a length of tubing, traditionally made from goat skin and approximately 3 metres long. It is covered in crocheted cotton or plaited threads, with a carved wooden mouthpiece (*mashrab*), sometimes inlaid with white metal. It is the mouthpiece that is handed from guest to guest, each person inhaling deeply, drawing the tobacco-smoke across the lighted coals, down and through the water and along the length of pipe. The gentle gurgling of the water resulting from this process provides a pleasant sound and evocative accompaniment to social gatherings.

The pipes are often used as an expression of wealth; each element can be highly decorated and the tinned metal or brass tray on which the pipe stands is often elaborately beaten and inscribed.

The *mada'ah al-kuz* is a simpler and less refined version of the above, using a pottery water container (*mada'ah*) in place of the *habba*. A half-metre length of cane, or a short length of rubber tubing, is used as a pipe and attached to the side opening of the *mada'ah*. This type of

27. Water-pipe base (*mada'ah*). Cat. 106

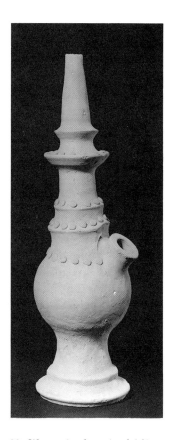

28. Water-pipe base (*mada'ah*). Cat. 107

water-pipe is easily portable, carried in a bag over the shoulder, and is largely used in the Tihamah, particularly by farmers, shepherds and itinerant workers.

Simple smoking pipes are made with a basic, hollow pottery pipe bowl, curved into a 'c' shape, and a length of cane. The water-pipe pieces in the Littlewood collection—a small number of water containers (*mada'ah*) and pipe-bowls (*buri*)—are not ornately decorated and, with the exception of some of the pipe-bowls, are made for the *mada'ah al-kuz*. The water containers are unglazed with simple painted, incised or raised decoration, and although a number of the pipe-bowls are glazed in the typical Haysi-style green/yellow lead glaze, they have few incised patterns. These glazed pipe-bowls are used for the burning and smoking of tobacco mixed with date syrup when the inside of the bowl is lined with tin before being filled with lighted coals and the tobacco.

Coffee

The national drink in Yemen, *qishr*, is made from the husks (outer shells) of coffee beans, combined with selected spices—cardamom, ginger or cinnamon—and sometimes sugar. Coffee (*bunn*) made from the bean (*safi*) is also drunk, but less often. There is a rich folklore associated with the history, cultivation and preparation of coffee (*qah-wah*) attesting to its great social and economic importance in Yemen in the past and today.

The coffee tree is not indigenous to South Arabia, and is said to have been introduced to Yemen from the highlands of Ethiopia around the turn of the fourteenth century. The beverage was first consumed by members of the Sufi religious sect who commented on an increased alertness and even rapture during their nightly devotional exercises as a result. Coffee-drinking took on something of a ceremonial character, perhaps because of its initial use amongst the religious élite, and the practice gradually spread to the rest of the population.

The coffee tree flourished in its new home. Coffee beans were established as an important export to Mecca and Cairo by the early sixteenth century, and to the Levant and Turkey soon after. The arrival of European merchants in the principal coffee-exporting port of Mokha (which lent its name, *mocha*, to a type of coffee) was significant for the coffee trade, as the custom of coffee-drinking spread to Europe and the rest of the world in the seventeenth and eighteenth centuries. However, the monopoly that Yemen and parts of Ethiopia had enjoyed in supplying the world's demand for coffee was broken by the western dealers who developed plantations in Ceylon, Java, the Caribbean and South America at the end of the seventeenth century and early eighteenth century. Coffee is still an important cash crop in Yemen, although it is now produced mainly for the home market, with some beans still exported for specialised use as a chocolate flavouring. Café society, as found elsewhere in the Middle East and Europe, never developed in Yemen where coffee is drunk exclusively in the home (E. I. New Edition, 'kahwa').

Qishr and bean coffee are prepared by women who pound and brew the coffee husks or beans for each day's needs in the morning, and usually have a pot ready and kept warm on a brazier (or in a vacuum flask), to be offered, along with tea, as soon as anyone arrives to visit the male or female members of the household. To make qishr, one handful of coffee husks, two handfuls of sugar, a teaspoon of ground ginger and half a teaspoon of cinnamon are covered in water, brought to the boil, covered and simmered for five minutes or so. However, the preparation of qishr and the balance of spices used is less strictly determined than for food, and some women display their individuality by flavouring it to their own taste. Qishr is seen as a refreshing beverage, effective in the relief of cares and anxieties, and is the essence of hospitality. In a few areas of Yemen, qishr is also served after lunch or dinner when it is seen as 'sealing' the meal.

Today coffee bean husks can be bought pre-pounded. Qishr is now often made in a metal teapot and served in Chinese-made porcelain tea cups (sini) which have largely (but not entirely) replaced the distinctive Haysi cups. Soft drinks are now sometimes offered to male visitors in place of qishr, but in much of Yemen qishr, coffee and tea are still the main drinks accompanying women's socialising.

The Littlewood collection contains a dish for roasting the bean husks, and coffee pots and cups. The unglazed but often burnished pot with a tall neck and one or two handles (of the style also used for water) is called jamanah. When serving qishr, stalks are stuffed in the spout of the pot to hold back the coffee grounds. Those that are partially glazed, bowl-shaped and with a simple spout are called masabb and are used for other more general purposes as well as for coffee. Examples of the latter type are also used for feeding babies, when they are known as mujru'a). The pots and cups catalogued here are decoratively and partially glazed in the yellow/green lead glaze typical of Hays; indeed the cups are often called haysi.

Toys and miscellanea

The few toys in evidence in Yemen are primarily made by children themselves from wire and scraps of rubbish. With the exception of western-style dolls which have recently appeared, toys made of pottery are possibly the only manufactured examples. Even so, the range of pottery toys in Yemen is small, incorporating miniature copies of water vessels and depictions of animals. One reason for the paucity of toys generally might be the short period of 'childhood' (as defined in western terms) and the early age at which children take on adult responsibilities in the home. Another might be the prohibition in Islam of the making of images or statues. Poverty is also a factor—the pottery toys do not last long.

Certain toys are made, bought and given at specified times of the year, especially in the month of Sha'aban before Ramadhan or at Muslim festivals. These include miniature versions of the highly decorative *sharbat al-'arus* water vessels described above, and pots with three bodies and a shared spout (see plate 3), twinned dishes and cups. Also to be found are assorted models, including representations of camels, swords and knives, palm trees and dhows (although certain of these are available throughout the year). Some of these have more recently been made out of sugar rather than clay.

The Littlewood collection contains pieces representing a rider on horseback, a camel and (possibly) an oryx. Interestingly, many of these are very similar to examples excavated in Yemen and found in the archaeological record in a number of locations in the Middle East. There is also a pottery model of a portable cradle of a type made of basketry with a leather base and wooden legs (see fig. 42). The mother hooks her arm through the arches of wood and carries the child to work with her, draping a piece of cloth over the arches of wood to shield the child. The two miniature pots in the collection may be examples of those made for Sha'aban or Muslim festivals. All the toys in the Littlewood collection are unglazed. Those which are lime-washed and decorated with the bright chemical colours of imported pen inks are typical examples of toys from Lahej.

A wheel-made and glazed goldsmith's crucible stands out as the only piece in the Littlewood collection used outside the domestic sphere. Sadly, no details on how the piece was used were collected. A curious and possibly unique piece in the collection is a pottery head of the first President of the Yemen Arab Republic after the overthrow of the Royalist Imamate in 1962 (see fig. 29).

29. Bust of a man representing Abdullah al-Sallal. Cat. 142

Clay in Yemen

Despite the variety and range of pots in the Littlewood collection, it is worth mentioning the pottery vessels and other clay objects from Yemen which Dr Littlewood was unable to collect due to their size or rarity; other items fell outside his sphere of interest because they were made from unfired clay or used outside the home.

The most significant clay items not represented in the collection are perhaps the sun-baked and fired bricks which are used to build the multi-storey houses in the highlands. The sources of clay for the bricks are the same as those for the household items described in the sections above, and the vast 'beds' where the clay bricks, earth mixed with water and sometimes straw, are left to dry in the open, are often situated close to the workshops and kilns of the potters (see fig. 30). However, the two crafts are entirely separate.

Ornate house decorations, often in the form of animals, are made from clay, baked in the sun and mounted above doorways, or applied and moulded to the walls when partially dry (see fig. 5). Fired but unglazed pipes and gutters are to be found in some areas, for example in the Hadramaut where Tufnell (1961) also reports seeing pottery balusters and spouts for irrigation. Littlewood (1963) observes that many of the tombs in the Hadramaut are marked by fired and inscribed clay funeral tablets.

Perhaps the most important but understandable omissions in the collection are the large, heavy cylindrical bread ovens (*tannur*) dis-

30. Clay bricks being moulded and laid out to dry in Mansuriyah, near Hodeidah. (Photo: Shelagh Weir, 1973–4)

cussed above. Also, Tufnell (1961) describes a baby's potty and bucket being produced by potters in Tarim; the potty was mounted on a stand with a handle, and the bucket, for milking goats and holding curds, had four handles from which the vessel could be suspended on a cord, and a spout. Flower pots for use in and around the home were particularly popular with the European community in Aden.

Some of the larger fired pottery pieces are particularly interesting. Chicken coops were made from large, open-topped, free-standing cylinders, similar in size and shape to the bread ovens, which were pierced with a number of ventilation holes. Two- and four-piece mounted beehives can still be seen in the Hadramaut and the Tihamah (Stone 1985), and large indigo dye vats are used in a number of regions (see plate 1).

Serjeant (1951) describes two fired pottery drums in use in the port of Balhaf in the Hadramaut in 1947; white parchment was stretched across both ends of the waisted cylinders and the instruments heated over a charcoal fire in a pottery brazier to tighten the skins before use. Littlewood has photographs of toy models of aeroplanes in clay which were made during his stay in Yemen, and Tufnell (1961) comments on children's models of horses and ibex, similar to the animal representa-

31. A potter's home in Mimdarah, near Shaykh Othman, with walls partly made of water storage jars. In the foreground is a small kiln, and to the far left two bread ovens (*tannur*).
(Photo: Mark Littlewood, 1960s)

tions in the Littlewood collection, and clay dolls made at Mimdara.

As noted above, many items of traditional Yemeni domestic pottery have been replaced by mass-produced plastic, metal and cheap imported porcelain alternatives. To some extent these carry out the same functions as their predecessors, and are simply more durable substitutes. In some cases, however, they are higher-status objects for conspicuous use in the consumption of key commodities; smart thermos flasks have replaced pottery water storage vessels when serving water to guests during the afternoon social gatherings, and ornate metal water-pipe bases have superseded pottery ones on similar occasions. The decline in demand for certain traditional pottery wares also reflects recent social change in Yemen and the adoption of western-style commodities and tastes.

It is those pottery items which have traditionally functioned in the more public social domain for the provision of hospitality, that have been most prone to replacement by higher-status alternatives. Those that play a key domestic role, often 'behind the scenes', have been more resistant to replacement, particularly if new products do not do the job as well and as cheaply. Coffee pots and cups, braziers, large water storage jars and bread ovens are all still produced and sold throughout Yemen today, though overall demand has declined. Incense burners are still widely used and have found a new market among the growing number of tourists who now visit Yemen. It is as if this item, of all pieces in the potters' repertoire, is being promoted as an acceptable 'craft' item. Indeed, a smart Sana'a hotel, converted from a traditional multi-storey house, has lamp bases made of pottery incense burners in its bedrooms.

Yemeni potters face an uncertain future. The older generation and the poor in rural areas still use a large number of pottery items in the home, but with growing modernisation the demand for such wares may steadily decrease. Littlewood commented on the decline of this centuries-old craft as early as the 1960s. We are, therefore, fortunate that he chose to make his collection when he did, to collect so widely, and to document so fully such an important area of Yemeni material culture.

Catalogue of the Littlewood Collection

Incense burners

1 Incense burner (*majmarah*)
'Cup' style with three exaggerated points around rim; unglazed and lime-washed, with dark red (slip) and black (ink) linear designs. Made in Hays, Tihamah. Purchased in Sanaa. H.16.2 cm.

1971As.7.4   (SEE FIG. 3)

2 Incense burner (*majmarah*)
'Cup' style with three projections from the rim and clay 'beads' attached to base of cup by cotton thread (unfired); unglazed and lime-washed, with linear designs in red and green ink. Made and purchased in Lahej. H.11 cm

1993As.11.12   (SEE FIG. 3)

3 Incense burner (*majmarah*)
'Covered' style with handle; unglazed and lime-washed, with linear designs in purple ink. Made and purchased in Lahej. H.16.2 cm

1966As.3.6

4 Incense burner (*majmarah*)
'Covered' style with handle; unglazed and lime-washed, with linear designs and triangles of colour in dark red and blue ink. Made and purchased in Lahej. H.15.8 cm

1966As.3.7   (SEE FIG. 3)

5 Incense burner (*majmarah*)
'Covered' style; unglazed and lime-washed, with linear designs in purple and red ink. Made in the Tihamah. H.17.5 cm

1993As.11.19

6–8 Incense burner (*majmarah*)
'Covered' style with loop at top; unglazed and lime-washed, with linear designs in red-brown slip. Made in Rahidah, between Kirsh and Taizz. Purchased in Aden (Crater Market). H.16 cm

1993As.11.8

Two further similar. H.15 cm

1993As.11.9 and 1993As.11.21

9 Incense burner (*majmarah*)
'Cup' style with loop at top; unglazed, with incised linear designs. Made in Taizz. H.15.5 cm

1993As.11.20

10 Incense burner (*majmarah*)
'Covered' style with handle (unfired?); unglazed and burnished, with pale-yellow slip, and floral and linear designs in red and green ink (?). Made in Dis or Shihr, east of Mukalla. Purchased in Seiyun, Hadramaut. H.11.4 cm

1965As.7.9   (SEE FIG. 22)

11 Incense burner (*majmarah*)
Square 'cup' style with four legs and flat base; unglazed and burnished, with pale-brown slip and linear designs in red ink. Made in Dis or Shihr, east of Mukalla. H.8 cm

1993As.11.16

PLATE 5 Coffee cups *(haysi)*.
(left) Cat.127 *(right)* Cat.128

PLATE 4 *(Previous page)* A potter
in Marrawah, near Hodeidah,
using the 'paddle and anvil'
technique. The pot is standing
upside-down and as the potter
walks around it backwards,
beating as he goes, he will
gradually close off its base.
(Photo: Shelagh Weir, 1973-4)

PLATE 6 Incense burner
(majmarah). Cat.30

12 Incense burner (*majmarah*)
'Cup' style, with handle and four projections from the rim; unglazed and burnished, with pale-brown slip and linear designs in red and green ink. Made in Dis or Shihr, east of Mukalla. H.9 cm

1993As.11.17   (SEE FRONT COVER, FIG. 22)

13 Incense burner (*majmarah*)
'Covered' style with two handles; lead glazed (dark yellow), with incised designs, laid-on strips of patterned clay, and surmounted with a 'crown'. Made in Hays, Tihamah. H.17.1 cm

This is an unusual piece, both in form and in its ornate decoration.

1966As.3.5   (SEE FIG. 18)

14 Incense burner (*majmarah*)
'Covered' style with handle; lead glazed (green). Made in Hays, Tihamah. H.15.3 cm

1971As.7.12

15 Incense burner (*majmarah*)
'Covered' style with handle; lead glazed (dark yellow). Made in Hays, Tihamah or by a Haysi potter based nearby. H.15.7

1971As.7.9

16 Incense burner (*majmarah*)
'Cup' style; unglazed, with impressed designs of stars. Made and purchased in Shaykh Othman. H.8.2 cm

1967As.3.7

17–22 Incense burner (*majmarah*)
'Cup' style with scalloped rim; unglazed, with impressed horizontal band and designs of stars. Made and purchased in Shaykh Othman. H.10.2 cm

1967As.3.8

Another similar, with impressed horizontal band and designs of stars and circles. H.11.4 cm

1967As.3.9   (SEE FIG. 17)

Another similar, with impressed horizontal band and designs of gridded circles. H.11.8 cm

1967As.3.10

Another similar, with impressed designs of flowers, leaves and flecks. Made and purchased in Lahej. H.11.5 cm

1993As.11.4

Two further similar, with impressed designs of flowers and flecks. Made and purchased in Lahej. H.11.5

1993As.11.5 and 1993As.11.6

Cats. 20–22 were made by Abdullah Sufian, uncle of Fitini Hazam, the main potter in Lahej.

23 and 24 Incense burner (*majmarah*)
'Covered' style; unglazed, with impressed horizontal bands and designs of stars, circles and ovals, two rows of small holes near the top, and surmounted with a bird. Made and purchased in Shaykh Othman. H.18.1 cm

1967As.3.11

Another similar, lime-washed and covered with powdered *kohl*. H.19 cm

1966As.3.23   (SEE FIG. 17)

25 and 26 Incense burner (*majmarah*)
'Covered' style with handle; unglazed and lime-washed, with linear designs in red ink, incised triangular shapes and surmounted with a bird. Made and purchased in Lahej. H.19 cm

1993As.11.10

Another similar, with linear designs in purple and green ink. H.18 cm

1993As.11.11

27 Incense burner (*majmarah*)
'Cup' style with four projections from the rim and a handle; unglazed, with pale-brown slip and linear designs in dark-brown slip. Made and purchased in Tarim, Hadramaut. H.6.9 cm

1965As.7.15

28 Incense burner (*majmarah*)
'Cup' style with three projections from the rim; unglazed and lime-washed, with stripes and spots in red and blue ink. Purchased in Lahej. H 7.5 cm.

1966As.3.8

29 and 30 Incense burner (*majmarah*)
'Cup' style with three projections from the rim and a handle; unglazed and burnished, with linear designs and spots in dark red 'dragon's blood', and six small holes pierced in the base and sides of the cup. Made on Socotra Island. Purchased in Aden (Ma'alla Harbour). H.9 cm

1993As.11.22

Another similar. H.11 cm

1993As.11.23   (SEE PLATE 6)

Water vessels

31 Water vessel (*ibriq* and *sharbat al-'arus*)
With handle and spout; unglazed and lime-washed, with linear designs in black, yellow and red-brown ink. Made and purchased in Suq al-Khamis (Khamis al-Wa'izat), Tihamah. H.27.3 cm

1967As.3.17   (SEE FIG. 32)

32. Cat. 31

32 Water vessel (*sharbat al-'arus*)
With four handles; unglazed and lime-washed with linear and floral designs in black and red-brown slip. Made in Hays or Jarahi, Tihamah. H.28.8 cm

1966As.3.28   (SEE FIG. 16)

33 Water vessel (*sharbat al-'arus*)
With handle; unglazed and lime-washed with linear designs in black, yellow and red-brown slip. Made in Hays, Tihamah. Purchased in Taizz. H.29 cm

1993As.11.55

34 Water vessel (*sharbat al-'arus*)
Similar to cat. 33, but with four handles and linear designs in black and stripes and patches in red-brown slip. Made in Hays, Tihamah. Purchased in Taizz. H.32 cm

1993As.11.56   (SEE FRONT COVER)

35 Water vessel (*sharbat al-'arus*)
Similar to cat. 33, but with three handles. H.24 cm

1993As.11.57

36 Water vessel (*sharbat al-'arus*)
Comprised of three pots sharing a single neck, with three handles; unglazed and lime-washed, with linear and 'leaf' designs in black and red-brown slip. Made in Hays, Tihamah. H.34 cm

1993As.11.58   (SEE PLATE 3)

37 Water vessel (*sharbat al-'arus*)
With two handles; unglazed and lime-washed, with linear designs in black and red-brown slip. Made and purchased in Suq al-Khamis (Khamis al-Wa'izat),Tihamah. H.22.8 cm

1967As.3.16   (SEE FIG. 16)

38 and 39 Water vessel (*sharbat al-'arus*)
With two handles; unglazed and lime-washed, with linear designs, spots and stars in black and red-brown slip. Made and purchased in Habil, near Lahej. H.36.5 cm

1966As.3.16

Another similar, with linear designs and circles in black ink. H.29.9 cm

1966As.3.17

40 Water vessel (*jarrah* or *kuz*)
Unglazed with red-brown slip and linear designs made up of raised 'blobs' of blue, red and white pigment. Made in Bajil, near Hodeidah. H.31.5 cm

This is an unusual piece that may have been made for a bride's 'trousseau' or for sale to tourists. Curiously the neck is blocked by a plate of clay pierced with five holes.

1993As.11.62

41 Water jug (*masabb*)
With handle, spout and rounded base; unglazed with painted linear designs in red-brown slip. Made in Al Bayda. Purchased in Makheras. H.25.4 cm

1965As.7.1

42 Water vessel (*jamanah?*)
With rounded base, ornate spout, handle and seven 'loops' on neck and spout; unglazed and burnished, with light-brown slip on rim of spout, incised dots, and raised lines, horizontal bands and circles over body and neck. Made in Mansuriyah, Tihamah. H.28 cm

1993As.11.59

43 Water vessel (*jamanah?*)
With rounded base, ornate spout and handle; unglazed and burnished, with raised horizontal bands around body and neck. Made in Mansuriyah, Tihamah. H.26 cm   (SEE FIG. 33)

1993As.11.60

Both cat. 42 and cat. 43 may have been made for a bride's trousseau.

33. Cat. 43

44 Water jug (*jamanah*)
With handle, spout and rounded base; unglazed and burnished. Made and purchased in Suq al-Khamis (Khamis al-Wa'izat), Tihamah. H.20.6 cm
1967As.3.12

45 Water jug (*ibriq*)
With handle and spout; unglazed and burnished. Made and purchased in Suq al-Khamis (Khamis al-Wa'izat), Tihamah. H.21 cm
1967As.3.13

46 and 47 Water vessel (*jarrah* or *kuz*)
With two handles and rounded base; unglazed and burnished. Made in Rahidah, between Kirsh and Taizz. Purchased in Tor al-Bahr (exact location unknown). H.22.9 cm

1965As.7.3

Another similar. Made and purchased in Rahidah between Kirsh and Taizz (?). H.27 cm

1993As.11.61

48 Water vessel (*jarrah* or *kuz*)
With tall neck; unglazed with incised linear designs. Purchased in Hodeidah and made nearby. H.30.2 cm

1971As.7.2

49 and 50 Water vessel (*jarrah* or *kuz*)
With two handles; unglazed with incised linear designs and raised and striped horizontal band. Made and purchased in Shaykh Othman. H.34.6 cm

1966As.3.27   (SEE FIG. 6)

Another similar, with incised linear designs and cross-hatching, and scalloped horizontal band. H.27.3 cm

1966As.3.26

Both cat. 49 and cat. 50 were made by Ahmed Salem Hasson, a Zabidi potter working in Shaykh Othman.

51 Water vessel (*jarrah* or *kuz*)
With two handles; unglazed with incised linear designs, cross-hatching, and raised and striped horizontal band. Purchased in Shaykh Othman. H.27.9 cm

1967As.3.21

52 Water vessel (*jarrah* or *kuz*)
Similar to cat. 51, but with four handles and lime-washed. Made and purchased in Lahej. H.32 cm

This piece was made by the mother of Fitini Hazam, the main potter in Lahej.

1993As.11.63

53 Water vessel (*jarrah* or *kuz*)
With two handles; unglazed with incised linear designs and four scalloped horizontal bands. Made in Shaykh Othman. Purchased in Shaykh Othman (?). H.34.9 cm

1965As.7.6   (SEE FIG. 6)

This piece would have most probably been made by a Zabidi potter.

54 Water vessel (*jarrah* or *kuz*)
With six handles (three down each side of the pot); unglazed with incised cross-hatched designs and five raised horizontal bands, four of which are indented. Made and purchased in Shaykh Othman. H.39 cm

1993As.11.64   (SEE FIG. 6)

55 Water vessel (*jarrah* or *kuz*)
With two handles and rounded base; unglazed and burnished, with incised linear designs. Made in Bayt al-Faqih (?), Tihamah. H.34.3 cm

This piece was made by a Zabidi potter.

1965As.7.4

56 Water vessel (*jarrah* or *kuz*)
With tall neck; unglazed with incised linear designs. Made by a potter from the Hadramaut. Made and purchased in Zinjibar. H.35.8 cm

1966As.3.24

57 Water vessel (*zir*)
With wide mouth; unglazed with red-brown slip. Made and purchased in Zinjibar. Made by a potter from the Hadramaut. H.87 cm

1966As.3.25

58 Water vessel (*jarrah* or *kuz*)
With handle, spout and rounded base; unglazed with incised linear and wave-like designs. Made and purchased in Shaykh Othman. H.35.9 cm

1967As.3.3

59 Water vessel (*jarrah* or *kuz*)
With rounded base; unglazed with incised linear designs. Made and purchased in Shaykh Othman. H.31 cm

1967As.3.6

60 and 61 Water vessel (*jarrah* or *kuz*)
With short neck and rounded base; unglazed with incised linear designs. Made and purchased in Shaykh Othman. H.41.3 cm

1967As.3.5

Another similar, with a tall neck and incised linear and wave-like designs. H.40 cm

1967As.3.4

62 Water vessel (*jahlah*)
With short neck; unglazed with incised linear designs and cross-hatched markings all over body of pot. Made in Mimdarah, near Shaykh Othman. Purchased in Aden (Crater Market). H.51 cm

1967As.3.35   (SEE FIG. 14)

63 Water vessel (*jahlah*)
With wide mouth; unglazed with incised linear designs. Made in Mimdarah, near Shaykh Othman. Purchased in Aden (Crater Market). H.37.5 cm

1967As.3.36   (SEE FIG. 34)

64 Water vessel (*jahlah*)
With short neck; unglazed with incised linear designs. Made in Mimdarah, near Shaykh Othman. Purchased in Aden (Crater Market). H.82 cm

1967As.3.37

65 Jug (*masabb*)
With handle and spout (unfired?); unglazed. Made in Turbah or Dhubhan area, near Taizz. H.15.9 cm

This jug may also have been used for making coffee or for feeding infants.

1967As.3.26

34. Cat. 63

35. Cat. 66

66 Jug (*masabb*)
With handle and spout; unglazed with pale-brown slip and lozenge designs and spots in dark-brown slip. Made and purchased in Tarim, Hadramaut. H.14.6 cm

1965As.7.8   (SEE FIG. 35)

36. Left Cat. 68, right cat. 67

67 Jug (*masabb*)
With handle, spout and rounded base; unglazed
with incised linear designs around the handle and
rim. Made near Hodeidah. Purchased in
Hodeidah. H.12.7 cms

1971As.7.1   (SEE FIG. 36)

68 Jug (*masabb*)
With handle and spout; unglazed and burnished
with red-brown slip and incised flecks. Made on
Socotra Island. Purchased in Aden (Crater
Market). H.23 cm

1965As.7.19   (SEE FIG. 36)

69 Seven jugs (*masabb*)
Each with a handle and spout, strung together
between two sticks with palm leaf(?) string;
unglazed and burnished with red-brown slip.

Made on Socotra Island. Purchased in Aden
(bought from a sailor in Ma'alla Harbour). L.95 cm

1967As.3.31a–g   (SEE FIG. 21)

Each jug seems to bear the word 'hope' in Arabic
(in its plural form). It is possible that this indicates a
blessing for their safe arrival in Aden from Socotra
Island. Alternatively it may be the name of the
maker and/or trader, to identify the pieces among
other goods on board the dhow.

70 Vessel
With handle and rounded base; unglazed. Made in
Turbah or Dhubhan area, near Taizz. H.16.5 cm

1967As.3.27

71 and 72 Vessel
With wide body and narrow neck; unglazed with
incised linear designs. Purchased in Ghayl
Bawazir, near Mukalla. H.18.4 cm

1967As.3.28

Another similar, with wide body. H.14 cm

1967As.3.29

73 Vessel
With lid; unglazed and burnished, with red-brown
slip and linear designs and spots in pale-brown
slip. Made and purchased in Tarim, Hadramaut.
H.55 cm

This is an unusual piece that may have been based
on a traditional Chinese jar.

1993As.11.71a–b   (SEE FIG. 24)

Food preparation and consumption

74 and 75 Cooking pot (*burmah*)

With two handles and rounded base; unglazed and burnished with incised stripes, and 'fire-cloud' or 'flashing' on the surface of the pot. Made and purchased in Suq al-Khamis (Khamis al-Wa'izat), Tihamah. H.24.1 cm

1967As.3.14 (SEE FIG. 37)

Another similar, with incised dots and stripes. The two handles are not perforated. H.12 cm

1967As.3.15 (SEE FIG. 37)

76 and 77 Cooking pot (*burmah*)

With two handles and rounded base; unglazed. Made and purchased in Shaykh Othman. H.20.9 cm

1967As.3.1

Another similar. H.17.5 cm

1967As.3.2 (SEE FIG. 37)

78–80 Cooking pot (*burmah*)

With handle, spout and rounded base; unglazed. Made in Dhala. Purchased in Aden or Shaykh Othman. H.15 cm

1965As.7.7

Another similar. H.11.5 cm

1993As.11.48

Another similar. H.23 cm
Littlewood private collection (SEE FIG. 2)

Cats. 78–80 are in the style of pieces made by Yemenite Jews.

37. From left: cats 74, 75, 77, 82

81 Cooking pot (*burmah*)
With rounded base and four raised 'handles';
unglazed and burnished with painted designs in
deep red 'dragon's blood'. The handles are not
perforated. Made on Socotra Island. Purchased in
Aden. H.20 cm

1993As.11.70

82 Cooking pot (*burmah*)
With two handles and rounded base; unglazed
with linear designs in red-brown slip. The handles
are not perforated. Made in Khawlan, near Ma'rib.
Purchased in Sanaa. H.11.5 cm

1971As.7.6   (SEE FIG. 37)

83 Cooking pot (*burmah*)
With handle and rounded base; unglazed with
pale brown slip and raised horizontal band. Made
and purchased in Rahidah, between Kirsh and
Taizz. H.13 cm

1993As.11.51

84 Cooking pot (*burmah*)
With handle and rounded base; unglazed with
pale red-brown wash, red-brown 'slashes' and
raised horizontal band. Made in north Yemen.
H.52 cm

1993As.11.52

85 Cooking pot (*burmah*)
With two 'handles', unglazed with red-brown and
pale brown slip and raised horizontal band. The
handles are not perforated. Purchased in Taizz.
H.14 cm

Pots similar to cat. 85 are used for cooking fish.

1993As.11.53

86 Platter (*malahhah*)
For making pancakes; unglazed. Made in Hays,
Tihamah.   Purchased   in   Shaykh   Othman.
D.42.5 cm

1966As.3.30

87–90 Bowl (*haradah?*)
Partially lead glazed (yellow). Made and purchased in Lahej. H.7.9 cm

1966As.3.10.

Another similar. H.14.1 cm

1966As.3.11

Another similar. H.10.7 cm

1966As.3.14

Another similar; partially lead glazed (dark yellow/
green). H.7 cm

1966As.3.15

91 and 92 Bowl (*haradah?*)
Partially lead glazed (yellow with green line
around rim). Made and purchased in Lahej.
H.7 cm

1966As.3.12

Another similar. H. 6.8 cm

1966As.3.13

93 Bowl (*sayniyyah*)
For soup and sour milk; partially lead glazed (dark
yellow/green) with raised design below rim on
outside. Made and purchased in Suq al-Khamis
(Khamis al-Wa'izat), Tihamah. H.11.8 cm.

1967As.3.23

94 Cup
For soup, milk and coffee; partially lead glazed
(dark yellow). Made and purchased in Suq al-
Khamis (Khamis al-Wa'izat), Tihamah. H.7 cm

1967As.3.22

95 Bowl (*haradah*)
For mixing food; partially lead glazed (yellow with
green line around the rim). Made and purchased in
Hays, Tihamah. H.15 cm

1966As.3.4

96 and 97 Bowl (*maqla*)
For mixing food; unglazed with incised flecks and
two raised horizontal bands. Made in Janbay'iyah,
near Hodeidah. H.13.5 cm

1993As.11.45   (SEE FIG. 25)

Another similar, with four 'handles'. The handles
are not perforated. H.17 cm

1993As.11.46   (SEE FIG. 25)

98 Bowl (*maqla*)
For mixing food; unglazed with pale-brown slip,
incised flecks and a raised horizontal band. Made
and purchased in Abara (exact location unknown),
near Ibb. H.10 cm

This example would have been used for mixing
flour.

1993As.11.47   (SEE FIG. 25)

99 Plate (*sahn*)
Partially lead glazed (yellow with green line
around the rim). Made in Hays or Mashrafah (exact
location unknown), Tihamah. H.8 cm

1967As.3.25

100 Bowl (*maqla*)
Unglazed with incised linear designs. Made in
Rawdah, near Sanaa. Purchased in Sanaa. H.6 cm

1971As.7.3

101 Vessel (oil jar?)
With two handles; unglazed with red-brown slip
and two bands in dark red-brown slip. Made and
purchased in Tarim, Hadramaut. H.11 cm

1993As.11.76

102 Brazier (*marbakh*)
With built-in grate, two handles, large pierced
ventilation hole and wavy rim; unglazed with
red-brown slip. Made and purchased in Tarim,
Hadramaut. H.12 cm

1993As.11.33

103 Brazier (*marbakh*)
With two handles and two horizontal projections
from rim; unglazed with pale-brown slip. Origin
unknown. H.13.5 cm

1993As.11.34

104 Brazier (*marbakh*)
With two handles, three large projections from
the rim and three small projections from the rim;
unglazed with broad bands of pale-, mid- and
dark-brown slip. Made and purchased near Taizz.
H.21.5 cm

1993As.11.35   (SEE FIG. 38)

38. Cat. 104

Smoking apparatus

105 **Water-pipe base** (*mada'ah*)
With two-tiered top spout; unglazed with pale-brown slip and linear designs in red-brown slip. Made in Rahidah, between Kirsh and Taizz. Purchased in Tor al-Bahr (exact location unknown). H.33 cm

1965As.7.2

106 **Water-pipe base** (*mada'ah*)
With three-tiered top spout and unperforated projection on upper tier; unglazed with pale-brown slip and linear designs and spots in red-brown slip. Made in Rahidah, between Kirsh and Taizz. Purchased in Aden (Crater Market). H.40.3 cm

1967As.3.30   (SEE FIG. 27)

107 **Water-pipe base** (*mada'ah*)
Unglazed with four rows of raised clay discs. Made and purchased in Ramadah, near Taizz. H.36 cm

1993As.11.73   (SEE FIG. 28)

108 **Water-pipe base** (*mada'ah*)
With three-tiered top spout; unglazed with incised linear designs. Purchased in Shaykh Othman. H.36.4 cm

1967As.3.19

109 **Water-pipe base** (*mada'ah*)
With short top spout; unglazed with incised linear designs. Purchased in Shaykh Othman. H.26.2 cm

1967As.3.20

110 **Pipe-bowl for water-pipe** (*buri*)
Lead glazed (dark yellow) with incised linear designs. Made and purchased in Lahej. H.12.2 cm

1966As.3.18

111 **Pipe-bowl for water-pipe** (*buri*)
With wavy rim; lead glazed (dark brown/black) with incised horizontal lines. Made in Hays, Tihamah. Purchased in Shaykh Othman. H.17 cm

1993As.11.36

112 **Pipe-bowl for water-pipe** (*buri*)
Flared with fluted rim; lead glazed (dark yellow) with incised linear designs. Made in Hays, Tihamah. Purchased in Shaykh Othman. H.16 cm

1993As.11.37

113 **Pipe-bowl for water-pipe** (*buri*)
Unglazed with red-brown slip and incised linear designs. Made in Rahidah, between Kirsh and Taizz. Purchased in Shaykh Othman. H.12 cm

1966As.3.19

114 **Pipe-bowl for water-pipe** (*buri*)
With fluted rim; unglazed with incised linear designs. Made and purchased in Shaykh Othman. H.16.2 cm

1966As.3.20

39. Cat. 115

115 **Pipe-bowl for water-pipe** (*buri*)
Unglazed, burnished and blackened with *kohl* with incised linear designs. Made and purchased in Shaykh Othman. H.14.2 cm

1966As.3.21   (SEE FIG. 39)

116 **Pipe-bowl for water-pipe** (*buri*)
With wavy rim; unglazed with red-brown slip and linear designs in pale-brown slip both inside and outside. Origin unknown. H.18.5 cm

1993As.11.38

117 and 118 **Pipe-bowl for water-pipe** (*buri*)
Unglazed with bands of incised dots and linear designs. Made and purchased in Hamra, near Lahej. H.8.5 cm

1993As.11.39

Another similar. H.8 cm

1993As.11.40

119 **Pipe-bowl for water-pipe** (*buri*)
Unglazed with dark-brown slip. Origin unknown. H.8.8 cm

1993As.11.41

120 **Pipe-bowl for smoking pipe**
Unglazed with incised horizontal lines. Made and purchased in Shaykh Othman. H.3.5 cm

1993As.11.44

Coffee

121 **Coffee pot** (*jamanah*)
With two handles, one above the other; unglazed with pale-brown slip, raised decoration and linear designs and spots in red-brown slip. Made in Khawlan, near Ma'rib. Purchased in Sanaa. H.19 cm

1971As.7.5

122–125 **Coffee pot** (*masabb*)
With spout; partially lead glazed (green/dark yellow). Purchased in Bayt al-Faqih, Tihamah. H.13.3 cm

1966As.3.1

Another similar. H.6.9 cm

1966As.3.2

Another similar. H.7.6 cm

1966As.2.1

Another similar, with no hole in the spout. H.4.4 cm

1966As.3.2a

126 **Coffee pot** (*masabb*)
With spout; partially lead glazed (green/dark yellow). Made in Hays or Mashrafah (exact location unknown), Tihamah. H.6.5 cm

1967As.3.24

127 **Coffee cup** (*haysi*)
Partially lead glazed (dark green) with incised linear designs. Made in Hodeidah. H.6.3 cm

This pot was made by a Zabidi potter.

1965As.7.5   (SEE PLATE 5)

128 Coffee cup (*haysi*)

Partially lead glazed (yellow with dark-green stripes). Made in Hodeidah (?). Purchased in Bayt al-Faqih, Tihamah. H.5.3 cm

1966As.3.3   (SEE PLATE 5)

129 Seven coffee cups (*haysi*)

Lead glazed (orange/green). Made in the Tihamah (?), probably in Hays. Purchased in Aden (Ma'alla harbour). H.4 cm

1971As.7.11a–g

130 Coffee cup

Unglazed and burnished, with red-brown slip and pale-brown slip around lip and base. Made and purchased in Tarim, Hadramaut. H.6.3 cm

1965As.7.11

131 Coffee roaster

With handle and nine projections around the rim; unglazed and burnished, with red-brown slip. Made and purchased in Tarim, Hadramaut. H.8 cm

1965As.7.14   (SEE FIG. 40)

40. Cat. 131

Toys

132 Child's toy depicting a rider on horseback

Unglazed and lime-washed, with linear designs in red and blue ink. Made and purchased in Lahej. H.8.5 cm

1966As.3.9

133 Child's toy possibly depicting a camel

Unglazed with red-brown slip on the body and spots, head and legs in pale-brown slip. Made and purchased in Tarim, Hadramaut. H 15.3 cm

1965As.7.12

134 Child's toy depicting an animal with two horns

Unglazed, with red-brown slip on the body, and spots, horns and legs in pale-brown slip. Made and purchased in Tarim, Hadramaut. H.11.4 cm

1965As.7.13

135 Child's toy depicting an animal with two projections on its back

Unglazed, with red-brown slip on the body and spots, head and legs in pale-brown slip. Made and purchased in Tarim, Hadramaut. H.14 cm

1965As.7.16

136 **Vessel**
With two handles; unglazed and lime-washed, with painted linear designs in red-brown and black slip. Made in Hays or Jarahi, Tihamah. H.17.2 cm

1966As.3.29 (SEE FIG. 16)

137 **Vessel**
With tall, narrow neck; unglazed and lime-washed with painted linear designs in red, black and yellow inks. Made and purchased in Suq al-Khamis (Khamis al-Wa'izat), Tihamah. H.19.2 cm.

1967As.3.18

138 **Teapot (ornamental? toy?)**
Unglazed with pale-brown slip and lines and dots in red-brown slip both inside and out. Made and purchased in Tarim, Hadramaut. H.9.5 cm

1993As.11.74a–b (SEE FIG. 41)

139 **Coffee cups (ornamental? toys?)**
Unglazed with pale brown slip and lines and dots in red-brown slip. Made and purchased in Tarim, Hadramaut. H.4 cm

1993As.11.75a–d (SEE FIG. 41)

140 **Model of a portable cradle**
With three legs, two holes in base and five sausage-shaped lengths extending upwards from base to form a handle; unglazed, with pale-brown slip and linear designs and spots in red-brown slip. Made and purchased in Tarim, Hadramaut. H.20 cm

1993As.11.18 (SEE FIG. 42)

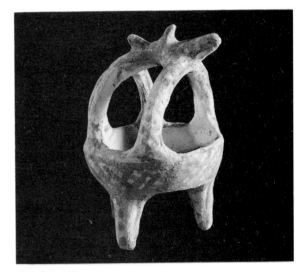

41. Teapot cat. 138, cups cat. 139

42. Cat. 140

Miscellaneous

141 **Goldsmith's crucible**
With spout; lead glazed (green) on inside only. Made in north Yemen. H.5.5 cm

1993As.11.77

142 **Bust of a man representing Abdullah al-Sallal**
Lead glazed (yellow and green). Made in north Yemen. H.10 cm

1993As.11.78 (SEE FIG. 29)

Select Bibliography

Arendonk, C. van. 1974. 'Kahwa' in the Encyclopedia of Islam, new ed., pp. 449–53.

Bonnenfant, P. and Centre d'Etudes et des Recherches sur l'Orient Arabes 1982. La Peninsule Arabique d'Aujourd'hui (2 vols.), Paris: Centre Nationale de la Recherche Scientifique.
1989. Les Maisons Tours de Sanaa: Texte et Photographes, Paris: Centre Nationale de la Recherche Scientifique.

Bornstein, A. 1974. Food and Society in the Yemen Arab Republic, Rome: Food and Agriculture Organization of the United Nations.

Central Statistical Organisation, Ministry of Planning and Development, The Republic of Yemen, 1991. National Population Strategy, 1990–2000.

Champault, D. 1974. 'Notes sur certains aspects de la céramique au Nord Yemen'. Objets et Mondes, XIV, 2, pp. 107–16.

Cooper, E. 1981. History of World Pottery (second edition), London: Batsford.

Costa, P. and Vicario, E. 1977. Arabia Felix: Land of the Builders, New York: Rizzoli International Publications.

Doe, D. B. 1963, 'Pottery sites near Aden'. Journal of the Royal Asiatic Society, pp. 150–62.

Encyclopaedia Britannica: A new survey of universal knowledge, 1955 Chicago, London etc. ('Dragon's blood'.)

Gettens, R.J. and Stout, G.L. 1942. Painting Materials, London: Chapman and Hall.

Groom, N. 1981. Frankincense and Myrrh: A study of the Arabian Incense Trade, London: Longman.

Hattox, R. S. 1985. Coffee and Coffeehouses: The Origins of a Social Beverage in the Medieval Near East, Near Eastern Studies No. 3, Seattle and London: University of Washington.

Keall, E. 1983. 'The dynamics of Zabid and its hinterland: The survey of a town on the Tihamah plain of North Yemen', World Archaeology, 14:3, pp. 378–92.
1993. (One man's Mede is another man's Persian; one man's coconut is another man's grenade.' Muqarnas, vol. 10, pp. 275–85.

Kirkman, J. 1976. City of San'a, London: World of Islam Festival Trust. (Catalogue to the 'Nomad and City' exhibition held at the Museum of Mankind, the Department of Ethnography of the British Museum.)

Lane, A. and Serjeant, R. B. 1948. 'Pottery and Glass Fragments from the Aden Littoral, with Historical Notes'. Journal of the Royal Asiatic Society, pp. 108–33.

Littlewood, M. 1963. Pottery in South Arabia. Aden Magazine (British Petroleum, no. 7).

Maclagan, I. 1993. Freedom and Constraint: The World of Women in a Small Town in Yemen. Unpublished PhD thesis.

Mason, R. B. and Keall, E. J. 1988. 'Provenance of Local Ceramic Industry and the Characterisation of Imports: Petrography of Pottery from Medieval Yemen'. Antiquity, 62, pp. 452–63.

Matson, F. R. (ed.) 1965. Ceramics and Man. Viking Fund Publications in Anthropology No. 41, Chicago: Aldine.

Pridham, B. R. (ed.) 1983. Economy, Society and Culture in Contemporary Yemen, London: Croom Helm and Centre for Arab Gulf Studies, University of Exeter.

Serjeant, R.B. 1951. *South Arabian Poetry* I; *prose and poetry from Hadramawt*, London: Taylor's Foreign Press.

Serjeant, R.B. *and* Lewcock, R. (eds.) 1983. *San'a': an Arabian Islamic City*, London: The World of Islam Festival Trust.

Stone, F. (ed.) 1985. *Studies on the Tihamah: The Report of the Tihamah Expedition 1982 and Related Papers*, Harlow: Longman.

Tufnell, O. 1960. 'A new approach to archaeology: The primitive potters of Mukalla ... Pots ancient or modern? Types of a craft unchanged for 3000 years'. *Illustrated London News*, March 12, pp. 438–9.
    1961. ' "These were the potters ..." Notes on the craft in Southern Arabia'. *Annals of Leeds University Oriental Society*, vol. II, 1959–61, pp. 26–36.

Van der Leeuw, S. E. *and* Pritchard, A.C. (eds.) 1984. *The Many Dimensions of Pottery: Ceramics in Archaeology and Anthropology*, Amsterdam: Universiteit van Amsterdam.

Varanda, F. 1981. *Art of Building in Yemen*, London: Aarp.

Weir, S. 1975. 'Some observations on pottery and weaving in the Yemen Arab Republic'. *Proceedings of the Seminar for Arabian Studies*, vol. 5, pp. 65–9.
    1985. *Qat in Yemen: Consumption and Social Change*, London: British Museum Publications.

Whitcomb, D. S. 1988, 'Islamic Archaeology in Aden and the Hadramaut' in Potts, D. T. (ed.) *Araby the Blest: Studies in Arabian Archaeology*, Copenhagen: CNI Publications (no. 7), pp. 177–263.

Glossary of Arabic Terms

bulbulah long tube attached to water-pipe
bulbul nightingale
bunn bean coffee
būrī pipe-bowl for water-pipe
burmah cooking pot; used mainly for meat but also for soup and porridge
dukhn finger millet flour
ḥabbah water-pipe base made of a decorated coconut (for *mada'ah Muneibari* q.v.)
ḥaraḍah partially glazed mixing bowl
ḥaysī coffee cup
ḥilbah fenugreek broth
ibrīq water vessel; for holding water for ritual ablutions
jaḥlah water vessel; medium-sized storage jar holding up to 20 litres (approx.)
jamanah water vessel or coffee pot
jarrah water vessel; small-sized jar holding up to one litre
kūz water vessel; small-sized jar holding up to one litre, used for drinking from, particularly at *qat* parties
mada'ah water container for water-pipe/water-pipe base
mada'ah al-kūz water-pipe (simple type)
mada'ah Muneibari water-pipe (ornate type)
majmarah incense burner

malaḥḥah pancake platter
maqlā dish or bowl
marbakh brazier
maṣabb general purpose or coffee pot; bowl-shaped with spout
mashab wooden pipe attached to water-pipe (for *mada'ah Muneibari* q.v.)
mashrab carved wooden mouthpiece, attached to water-pipe
mujrū' bowl for feeding babies
nūrah lime-wash
qahwah Arabic term for coffee
qāt Arabic term for *Catha edulis* Forssk.
qishr husk coffee
quṭb long stem attached to water-pipe (for *mada'ah Muneibari* q.v.)
ṣāfī coffee bean and drink made from it
ṣaḥn plate
ṣīnī Arabic term for Chinese-made porcelain tea-cups
ṣayniyyah bowl for soup and sour milk
sharbah water vessel
sharbat al-'arūs bridal water vessel
tafritah women's afternoon gathering
tannūr bread oven
zīr water vessel; largest storage jar holding up to 50 litres (approx.)